When There is **H.O.P.E**

Healing

Overcomes

Painful

Events

By

Bridgette M. Alfred

When There is H.O.P.E
© 2021 by Bridgette M. Alfred

All rights reserved. No portion of this publication may be reproduced, stored in a retrieval system, or transmitted in any form or by any means–electronic, mechanical, photocopying, recording, scanning, or other–except for brief quotations in critical reviews or articles, without the prior written permission of the publisher.

Published in Hampton, VA, by Fruition Publishing Concierge Services. Fruition Publishing Concierge Services is a division of Alesha Brown, LLC.

Fruition Publishing Concierge Services can bring authors to your live event. For more information or to book an event, visit Fruition Publishing Concierge Services at

www.FruitionPublishing.com

ISBN: 978-1-954486-17-1 Paperback

ISBN: 978-1-954486-18-8 eBook

Library of Congress Control Number: 2021912957

DEDICATION

I dedicate this book to the loving memory of my ninety-five year old mother, Mamie L. Stewart, who has transitioned from earth to Heaven. My mother started me on my spiritual journey and was a living testimony of Hope as she pressed through health issues the last two years of her life.

Table of Contents

CHAPTER 1 A LIFE FULL OF BETRAYALS 7

Biblical Characters for Chapter One..**47**
    Raynelle, Esther, and Tamar 47
    The Story of Esther..48
    The Story of Tamar..51
    Lauretta and Leah 53
    The Story of Leah 54
    Joseph, Hosea, and Samson...56
    The Story of Hosea 57
    The Story of Samson 57
    Gwendolyn, Delilah, and Herodias...59
    The Story of Delilah..59
    The Story of Herodias 61
    Andre, Alston, Salome, and Amnon 62
    The Story of Salome..62
    The Story of Amnon 63

CHAPTER 2 UNEXPECTED DESTINY 65

Biblical Characters For Chapter Two **99**
    Aunt Lottie And Jochebed 99
    The Story of Jochebed 99
    Uncle Claude And Abraham 101
    The Story of Abraham 101
    Uncle James and Mordecai 104
    The Story of Mordecai 105
    Charles Duplantier, Ahab, and Haman..106
    The Story of Ahab 106
    The Story of Haman 107

CHAPTER 3 CHANGED HEART 109

Biblical Characters For Chapter Three..**129**
    Grandma Louise And Miriam 129
    The Story of Miriam 129
    Grandpa Luke And Caleb 130
    The Story of Caleb 131

CHAPTER 4 THE ACADEMY CHRONICLES 133

Biblical Characters For Chapter Four 157
   Amber, Athaliah, And Potiphar's Wife 157
   The Story of Athaliah 157
   The Story of Potiphar's Wife 158
   The Story of Gideon 159

CHAPTER 5 SECRETS EXPOSED 163

Biblical Characters For Chapter Five 199
   David Williams And Boaz 199
   The Story of Boaz 199
   Derek And Lot 200
   The Story of Lot 200
   Eddie Haynes And Judas Iscariot 201
   The Story of Judas 202
   Andre and Absalom 203
   The Story of Absalom 204

CHAPTER 6 SECOND CHANCE FOR LOVE 205

Biblical Character For Chapter Six 235
   Pastor Redding, Elijah, And Elisha 235
   The Story of Elijah 235
   The Story of Elisha 237
   Brenda Redding And The Prodigal Son 239
   The Story of the Prodigal Son 240
   Daniella, The Shunammite Woman, and Hannah 241
   The Story of the Shunammite Woman 241
   The Story of Hannah 243

Introduction

We all need Hope because life can be hard. Sometimes, we have to endure a *bad day*. Other times, we face heartache. No amount of tears can bring it to an end. Most of us face difficult times more often than we would like. Yet, as difficult as life can be, Hope guides us and gets us through the storms of life. Take away Hope and even the small things crush us.

As we look at the big picture in our world, we see hopeless situations. The news regularly blasts us with stories of the harmful and even evil situations people endure. Abuse, divorce, murder, war, famine, rape, and natural disasters torment our lives and shred our broken world. Beyond the unexpected disasters that make the news, we're wounded by the daily actions of others who never get headlines but hurt us deeply.

Hope is a feeling of expectation and desire for a certain thing to happen. Hope is an optimistic attitude of mind that is based on an expectation of positive outcomes, related events, and circumstances in one's life or the world at large. Hope as a strong certainty that what God has promised in the Bible is true, has occurred, and or will be in accordance with God's sure Word.

God is called "the God of Hope" which means He is the source of all real Hope. If we are going to have Hope it must come from Him for He alone has the power to give it. If this is true, we begin to wonder how God can allow bad things to happen to good people. Is this how God intended us to live? Is this the kind of life He created us for? Thankfully, the answer is no. The Bible tells us the true story of how God created us and our world, how we fell away from His original design, and what He did to heal our brokenness. It offers Hope because we discover that God is in the business of restoring us to His beautiful original intentions.

This book, When There is H.O. P. E. (Healing Overcomes Painful Events) was not written as a self-help book. Instead, it is a testament/testimony to show that the same events/experiences we have right now are similar to those in the Word of God. This book's cover contains specific symbolism for the Christian journey through life: The anchor represents a grounding (Hope) securely connected to the cross (Faith). The heart symbol (Love) represents love and affection for others. The symbols of Hope, Faith, and Love represent the three theological virtues that God puts into the believer's soul. We must live our lives according to these virtues to be worthy of eternal life.

The Hope of eternal life endures even while the believer struggles with life's challenges. The worldly hope is no hope at all, but Hope in Christ is a firm and secure anchor of the soul. Hebrews 6:19 describes the Hope we have in Christ. "We have this Hope as a sure and steadfast anchor of the soul, which enters the Inner Place behind the veil."

The soul, according to the biblical definition, is the mind, the will, and the emotions. An anchor serves to hold a boat firmly. Therefore, when the winds of life are blowing, and the waves are rolling, and circumstances surrounding your purpose and life aren't going how you planned, Hope in God is an anchor to keep your mind, your will, and your emotions steady.

There is, however, a very interesting thing about having one's mind, will, and emotions anchored in the Hope that is Christ. If you believe you have no anchor—even though you do—you will respond as if the wind and waves of life are overtaking you and that you are perishing. When you could have peace, you'll be panicking, fretting, and feeling hopeless. Even though God has said that you have a firm and secure Hope, you will respond like you have no anchor. There are some things that God has given that are undeniably yours, but you will only experience the joy and peace knowing they are yours by believing. You have a Hope that is steady and secure.

The cross, representing Faith, symbolizes the believer's deep trust in that all God has revealed is true. The cross of Faith is important because believers are expected to share with others their faith in God's truth. No matter how rough life gets, the believer is always attached to the source of Faith.

Significance of the cross is told by the authors of the Gospel by telling us that the Lord Jesus spoke of the cross before His death (Matthew 10:38; Mark 10:21; Luke 14:27) as a symbol of the necessity of full commitment for those who would be His disciples. However, the major significance of the cross after Jesus' death and resurrection is its use as a symbol of Jesus' willingness to suffer for our sins (Philippians 2:8; Hebrews 12:2) so that we might be reconciled (2 Corinthians 5:19; Colossians 1:20) to God.

The cross, then, is the symbol of Jesus' love, God's power to save, and the thankful believer's unreserved commitment to Christian discipleship. To those who know the salvation that Christ gained for us through His death, it is a wondrous cross indeed.

The heart symbol represents *love* and affection for others. Believers strive to love God and to love others as God loves them. Love symbolizes the desire to love everyone, including one's enemies, neighbors, and the poor. The three symbols are bound by love. Love cannot be achieved without faith and hope because love is love for all. In theology, the cross with an anchor, and the heart are interlocked.

The heart is the inner self that thinks, feels, and makes decisions. In the Bible, the word heart has a much broader meaning than it does to the modern mind. The heart is that which is central to a person. Nearly all of the references to the heart in the Bible refer to the same aspect of human personality.

The source of life is rendered a heart (Ephesians 6:6), *doing the will of God from the heart.* In the Bible, all emotions are experienced by the heart: love and hate (Psalm 105:25; 1 Peter 1:22), joy and sorrow (Ecclesiastes 2:10; John 16:6), peace and bitterness (Ezekiel 27:31; Colossians 3:15), and fear (Genesis 42:28).

The thinking processes are said to be carried out by the heart. This intellectual activity corresponds to what would be called the mind in English. Thus, the heart may think (Esther 6:6), understand (Job 38:36), imagine (Jeremiah 9:14), remember (Deuteronomy 4:9), be wise (Proverbs 2:10), and speak to itself (Deuteronomy 7:17). Decision-making is also carried out by the heart. Purpose (Acts 11:23), intention (Hebrews 4:12), and will (Ephesians 6:6) are all activities of the heart.

Finally, the heart often refers to someone's true character or personality. Purity or evil (Jeremiah 3:17; Matthew 5:8), sincerity or hardness (Exodus 4:21; Colossians 3:22), and rebelliousness (Jeremiah 5:23) all describe the heart or true character of individuals. God knows the heart of each person (1 Samuel 16:7). Since people speak and act from their hearts, they are to guard them well (Proverbs 4:23; Matthew 15:18–19). The most important duty of anyone is to love God with the whole heart

(Matthew 22:37). With the heart, a person believes in Christ and so experiences both love from God and the presence of Christ in the heart (Romans 5:5; 10:9–10; Ephesians 3:17).

The main character in this book is a woman by the name of Raynelle Angel Young. Raynelle's character helped her to endure the many significant life-changing events throughout her life. Through Raynelle's many encounters, she displayed a strong will and independent mindset. Many times she was knocked down but not out. Each season of her life, she had someone to encourage or motivate her to press on and not quit. You might lose a few battles, but you only lose the war if you wave a white flag and surrender. During Raynelle's many adversities (sibling betrayal, mother abandonment, father's murder, husband's infidelity, etc.), she persevered with supernatural inner strength.

During life's journey, we have our valley lows and mountain highs. How we approach them makes all the difference. Due to human nature, we often attempt to solve our problems but only make them worst. Studying the Bible through its characters and learning about the lives of the people portrayed in the Bible can be a fascinating endeavor for several reasons. First, many of the Bible's characters are famous, and they have found permanent places in the popular Western imagination. The Bible's characters also show positive virtues that can be imitated. "What has been is the same as what will be, and what has been done is the same as what will be done; there is nothing new under the sun." (Ecclesiastes 1:9)

However, the Bible does not gloss over evil either. There are plenty of villains in the Bible. Interestingly enough, even the Bible's heroes are shown with their flaws. The very realism with which the Bible presents its heroes and villains is a strength. The

Bible shows God accomplishing many great things, using people who were not models of virtue. Rather, God used ordinary people. In today's complex and challenging world, that lesson can be comforting and encouraging.

This book can be used as a resource of interesting characters, many of whom are important in Western culture. Some readers will enjoy it for more personal, spiritual reasons given a study of characters to be learned from. Their stories are examples to be imitated or avoided. For all readers, however, it should prove to be a worthwhile book.

When There Is H.O.P.E. (Healing Overcomes Painful Events) is a work of fiction. In any instance where real people, events, establishments, organizations, or locales appear, they are used fictitiously. All other elements of the novel are drawn from the author's imagination.

Chapter 1

A Life Full of Betrayals

My name is Raynelle Angel (Young) Hendrix. I'm fifty-two years old, married to a wonderful man, Dan, and have one daughter, Michele Charlotte. I am the only child born from the marriage between Joseph Otis Young and Lauretta Ann (Rowell) Young. I do have twin half-brothers, Andre and Alston, who are a product of a very complicated relationship my father had before his marriage to my mother. I will talk more about them shortly.

Lately, I have been reflecting on the early years of my life. It took me a long time to feel content with myself. Like so many others, I had a very difficult childhood. Here's my story.

Recently, the second most influential member of my family died. This family member was my Aunt Charlotte, who was affectionately called Aunt Lottie by everyone. The world's standards wouldn't consider Aunt Lottie's appearance to be beautiful, but she was an incredible woman with an inner beauty that made up for any outward beauty.

Aunt Lottie would listen sincerely whenever someone was talking to her. She was an inspiration to everyone that knew her. Aunt Lottie had a lot of heartaches throughout her life also. She reminded me numerous times not to let the disappointments of my past dictate my future or destiny. Aunt Lottie was a firm believer that for whatever test or trial someone goes through, there is a testimony to share, encourage, and give hope to someone else. Many times, Aunt Lottie inspired and challenged me to go beyond my comfort zone.

Chapter 1 : A Life Full of Betrayals

Growing up in Washington, D.C., my parents and I lived on top of the grocery store and café that my Uncle Claude and Aunt Lottie owned in a small neighborhood. My father, aunt, and uncle had this agreement that they would open the store and he would close it at night. This arrangement was good for my parents because they constantly argued. Papa did take a break from the store when it was time for me to go to bed so he could say good night.

Where we lived had two bedrooms, a living room, a dining room, and an open kitchen with a door to a deck. My parents had a sitting room with a walk-in closet in their bedroom. We shared a bathroom. It was very modest with used furniture. My mother hated our living arrangements. She constantly pestered my father to buy us a house. He said, "I'm saving up for one." I could tell by her tone that she didn't believe him.

The café side of the store was called Café New Orleans. From the moment you arrived, you would be greeted and taken care of by Aunt Lottie. Café New Orleans was a natural fabric of the community. The copious space had a homey atmosphere—a cozy living-room feel. Customers would spend a morning gazing out admiringly watching Stewart Avenue traffic from the big bay window. Contemporary New Orleans cuisine was offered with innovative dishes that were as eye-catching as they were delicious.

The café had seasonal menus that changed based on the ingredients available for that time. The succulent, mouth-watering food was served in surroundings that could complement any number of moods. There was just enough space for fifteen small tables. Each table had candles on top of white tablecloths, rustic natural brick walls, and bistro chairs that gave you an inviting feeling and an upscale ambiance. Sometimes couples had a romantic evening for two.

The café was colorful enough for an adventurous get-together and approachable enough for nothing more than a relaxing evening made memorable by exceptional food and drink. During the summer months, tables were added on the adjoining outdoor patio, which helped when there was a waiting list for seats.

Aunt Lottie and Uncle Claude had moved to Washington, D. C. when he got stationed at the Thomas Parran Jr. Army Hospital. Uncle Claude was a field surgeon and this was his last duty station before retirement. They liked the area so that's why they bought the grocery store and café. Hard work ran in the family and Aunt Lottie needed something to occupy her time. Aunt Lottie ran the café while Uncle Claude and my father ran the grocery store. The store hours were 10:00 a.m. to 8:00 p.m. Monday thru Saturday. The store was closed on Sundays.

Uncle Claude and Aunt Lottie lived in a row house a few blocks away. Aunt Lottie was the best cook ever. People came from miles around just to eat her spicy jambalaya, gumbo, beignets, and bread pudding. They made everyone feel welcomed. I learned that Aunt Lottie gave you her words of wisdom whether you asked for them or not.

My earliest childhood memories are filled with a lot of yelling between my parents. This didn't change until a very significant event happened to me. When I was about three years old, I had a high fever and sore throat. I remember crying so hard because my mother had taken my bottle of milk out of my reach. My father was screaming at my mother "to give the bottle back to me."

Chapter 1 : A Life Full of Betrayals

My mother screamed back, "I told you not to give it to her!"

"Why not?" he asked.

"She's biting off the bottle nipples and I don't have any more in the house."

"How long does it take for the medicine to start to work?" My father asked.

"Ray should calm down soon," she answered. My mother tried to get me to drink from a cup. I pushed it away.

At that moment, I felt alone. To make things worse, there was a thunderstorm outside and I was so afraid. I believe that children are the most helpless members of the human race, depending upon others for food, physical safety, and emotional comfort. They cannot demand these rights. Thoughtless parents often abuse and neglect them.

Well, abuse and neglect were what I was feeling during this first disappointment in life. A child has the right to be loved and accepted. A child can detect a lack of compassion and affection very early in life.

My father finally came over and picked me up. He started rocking me and singing softly. He had written me a song to celebrate my birth and he sang it a lot of times to calm me down. This was definitely one of those times. He had titled the song "My Angel Ray."

When I was eight years old, my father announced we were taking our first trip as a family from Washington, D.C. to New Orleans, Louisiana. New Orleans is where my father and Aunt Lottie were originally from. We had never been on a vacation as a family before. This announcement made my mother mad for three reasons—the place we were going to, that we were spending the money to buy a house and the reason why we were going.

My father had twin sons from a previous relationship and it was their twelfth birthday. My mother blurted out, "We have been married for eight years, and you haven't taken us anywhere. We didn't even go on a honeymoon because you didn't want to miss work. But as soon as your former lover calls, we are off to New Orleans! You have never even seen your sons before!"

In anger, he reminded her, "I have their pictures."

"You know what I mean! You haven't ever seen them in person."

"That's not my fault and you know that!" My father bellowed back. "Why do you care the reasons why we are going?"

My mother always knew what to say to get my father angry. My father complained to my mother that any place that she wanted to go involved flying. Papa cried out, "You know I don't fly."

My mother barked back, "That's your justification for just being cheap."

My father insisted, "Every Sunday Ray and I go out. You never want to go with us."

My mother talked between gritted teeth, "There are more places to go than to parks, the zoo, and the Baltimore harbor."

Papa responded by saying, "You are getting a free trip now. It's your choice whether you go with us or not."

So, a month later on a Tuesday at 9:00 a.m., we took the Ellipse train from Union Station in Washington D.C. to Louisiana. We took a train because my father was terrified of flying. His parents had been killed in a plane crash, so there would be no flying ever for our family.

I was so excited. I sat by the window the whole time. I didn't want to miss a thing. I abstained from eating, sleeping, and using the bathroom until the last minute. It was a long trip. It took approximately twenty-six hours to get to Louisiana by train.

My father showed his extravagance by reserving the Elite sleeping accommodations, which was a suite with two bedrooms and a bathroom with a shower. The dining car served a variety of meals cooked by a chef. The exuberant conductor recited some history of each state as we passed through.

I thought it was fascinating when we crossed from Georgia to Alabama because the time zone changed. We traveled from the Eastern time zone to the Central time zone. The conductor spoke over the intercom system to remind the passengers to change their watch to one hour back.

We arrived on Wednesday around 11:00 a.m. New Orleans is known by several names: America's Most Interesting City, the Crescent City, the Big Easy, or just Nawlins. New Orleans has an abundant mix of jazz, nightlife, world-class restaurants, architecture, and history. The train station was located next to the construction of what would be the massive Louisiana Superdome which would become the largest fixed dome structure in the world.

Aunt Debra, one of my father's sisters, met us at the train station. Aunt Debra was five years older than my father. When I saw her it was like looking at a female version of my father. Aunt Debra was very tall for a woman and she was also slim like my father. Her hair was brown—perfectly styled—and she wore a beautiful purple silk dress. She batted her eyelashes a lot when she talked.

Aunt Debra hugged my father first and then he introduced my mother and me. When she hugged me, I thought, "This woman is so strong."

My father gathered all our bags together and put them in Aunt Debra's car. She drove a black Cadillac Fleetwood Eldorado convertible. I had never seen a car like this before. I asked Aunt Debra, "Could we drive with the top down?" Aunt Debra was delighted to put the top down for me. She instructed my father to drive while she and I sat in the back so we could get acquainted. My mother sat in the front passenger seat. The plan was for us to stay at the Duplantier mansion with my two brothers and their mother. Of course, this news didn't go well with my mother.

I announced that I was hungry. Aunt Debra suggested we stop at a diner before we drove to the Duplantier mansion. My parents rode in silence to the diner, which was very refreshing.

Eating at a diner was another new experience for me. The diner had white columns and a neon sign out front. It had no available tables, so we sat on stools at the counter. My father sat by Aunt Debra and I sat on the other side of her while my mother sat by me.

Aunt Debra was so different from my father. She started spinning around on the stools and I joined her. My father had to tell us to stop when the waiter with a bow tie arrived to take our orders. The menu included burgers, omelets, and milkshakes. My father ordered, "A double patty cheeseburger with Cajun fries and a glass of water." Aunt Debra only wanted a pistachio milkshake. I told her, "That's my favorite ice cream flavor too!" She remarked, "Great minds think alike!" and winked at me. I ordered, "A chili omelet and pecan pie à la mode for dessert." My mother ordered, "A house salad with oil and vinegar on the side and a glass of water." This was the first time my mother said a word since arriving at the diner.

Aunt Debra had never been married and she had no children. She worked as a nurse for a senior assisted living facility and adult medical daycare called Magnolia Estates. I asked Aunt Debra, "Why didn't you ever get married?" Aunt Debra explained, "I never found the right man," she chuckled. "I like going out and having fun."

I asked her, "What do you like to do for fun?"

Aunt Debra started moving around singing, "I love dancing, especially on Saturday nights. I'm hard-pressed to find a joint that's rocking with live music. From Frenchmen Street to Bourbon Street, musicians gear up to play some of the world's most famous jazz, zydeco, and blues music."

I told Aunt Debra, "I've heard of jazz and blues music, but I never heard of zydeco music."

"Zydeco can be traced to the music of enslaved African people from the 19th century. Zydeco is often considered the Creole music of Louisiana."

"Zydeco was initially sung only in Louisiana French or Creole, but since the 20th century, zydeco often incorporates a blend of swamp pop, blues, and or jazz as well as Cajun music." Aunt Debra claimed to me, "When you get older, I'll stay young so we can party together!"

I yelled, "That would be fine with me!"

"What do you like to do for fun?"

"I love to read books."

"What's the fun in just reading books?"

"I can imagine being at the place I'm reading about."

Aunt Debra took my face in her hands. "Raynelle, you are too young to be so serious. You need to stop being so serious or you will grow up dull and boring like my stuffed shirt of a brother." She winked at me again. Papa spoke up.

"I heard that Debra, and I'm not dull and boring."

Aunt Debra retorted, "When is the last time you went out and had some fun?"

My mother commented, "Never."

"I have too many responsibilities to think about having fun."

"That's my point," Aunt Debra said. She changed the topic.

"Are you excited to meet your brothers?"

"Yes. I miss not having siblings, especially during my birthday. I don't have a lot of friends."

I was tall and slender like my parents. Most boys were intimidated by my height.

"The girls are cruel and tease me because I usually answer all the questions first in class. The kids in my neighborhood are not around for my birthday because it's in June and they all go away for the summer."

Aunt Debra exclaimed, "I am so sorry to hear that."

I liked talking to Aunt Debra. She had a sense of humor.

"What made you decide to be a nurse at Magnolia Estates?"

"Aunt Lottie and Aunt Rebecca taught me to give back to the community. Growing up watching Aunt Lottie was the perfect example of love and she impacted my life solely because of her spiritual beliefs. Aunt Lottie's kindness and compassion for people was her legacy that inspired others to live in the same way. When I became an adult, I couldn't show the love I had for Aunt Lottie and Uncle Claude because they had moved to Washington, D.C."

Until that moment, I had forgotten my father and his two sisters were not raised together. Aunt Debra went on.

"Doing good to others comes back to you. Two of my patients unexpectedly left monies to me in their wills. I was able to pay cash for that beautiful car you rode in and my house in the French

Quarter. I converted my large house into a boarding house for people who are struggling and need somewhere to live."

"Aunt Debra, can you share some stories about the residents at Magnolia Estates?"

"There was a resident, Mrs. Jones, who they nicknamed the creeper. Every day Mrs. Jones would arrive by bus at the facility, walk a short distance, and announce she was ready to go home. The bus driver had to trick her into thinking that the bus to go home was at the back door of the facility."

"Sometimes, Mrs. Jones impersonated being a football player dodging the staff like she was trying to make a touchdown. She also would turn her wig crooked and talk smart remarks to everyone. Mrs. Jones really loved the attention. She would dance around on her tiptoes and yell *woo hoo*!"

I begged Aunt Debra, "Please, tell me another story."

"There was a hairstylist who came in once a week to do the resident's hair and nails and took care of other grooming as needed. There was a resident named Mrs. Jenkins who had been in a car accident and had an abusive husband. Mrs. Jenkins would stand at the door when the hairstylists came and looked at everyone getting their service done. She always wanted her hair done, but her husband never sent money to pay for it. The facility's staff felt sorry for her, so they took up a collection to pay for Mrs. Jenkins to receive a makeover. After the makeover, Mrs. Jenkins looked like a different person. The staff and other residents complimented her and it changed her self-esteem."

I told Aunt Debra that her stories were very funny and that I would like to visit Magnolia Estates before we went home. Aunt Debra said she would ask my father.

Once we completed our lunch, we piled back into Aunt Debra's car to drive to the Duplantier Mansion which was a short distance from the diner. It was an extravagant, luxuriously renovated historic 1830s masonry mansion in the elegant Garden District of New Orleans. The long entrance was enclosed by an iron fence, a professional and manicured landscape of sixteen acres, and a four-car garage. The mansion had beautiful wraparound porches and a spacious patio with an eight-foot swimming pool. The large private courtyard was flanked on one side by a high brick wall and framed on the other side by a separate two-story guest house that had private parking for two cars.

"I am not staying here," my mother proclaimed very loudly.

"But this was the plan!" My father exclaimed.

"It was your plan with no consideration for my feelings!"

Aunt Debra chimed in. "I know how she feels; this house is very intimidating." Aunt Debra suggested that my mother stay with her because a tenant moved when she got married recently.

"I want to stay with Momma!" I chimed in.

Papa asked me, "Ray don't you want to meet your brothers?"

"I do want to meet them, but I want to stay with Momma."

"It is long overdue for you to meet your brothers," my mother told me. "It will be rude to hurt their feelings on their birthday.

Ray, you wouldn't want anyone to disappoint you on your birthday."

I was thinking that I get disappointed all the time but I said nothing. There was going to be a big birthday party on Saturday to celebrate my brothers' birthday. This would be my first time seeing my brothers other than in the pictures my father had shown me. I knew that I couldn't win this discussion.

Aunt Debra got out of the car to help my father get our bags. "Men do not think like women! Little brother, I knew this would happen, but I had to mind my own business."

"Since when?"

"Don't take your frustrations out on me, Joseph. Did you at any time include Lauretta in planning this trip?"

"What, are you a marriage counselor now?"

"No, I just know how you are. I have dated men like you. You get so domineering and always have to be in charge and have things done your way. Men never think that women can make decisions without them."

My father ignored her last comment and got our bags from out of the car. I quickly got out of Aunt Debra's car. My mother just rolled her eyes at my father as Aunt Debra drove off. I didn't even say goodbye to my mother.

When I looked up at the mansion, I saw two pairs of eyes and then another pair appear behind a curtain. I guess they got a good look at the show my parents put on. My father rang the doorbell.

Chapter 1 : A Life Full of Betrayals

The doorbell played some type of fancy song. I heard loud footsteps running and shouting, "We got it, we got it!"

When my brothers opened the door, they were nothing like what I expected. Every set of twins I ever saw were identical. However, my brothers were fraternal.

Andre Charles Duplantier was the oldest and at least two inches taller than his twin brother. His hair was wavy dark brown and he wore it in a ponytail. Andre's eyes were also dark brown with thick eyebrows and lips, a wide nose, and an oval-shaped face. We both had the same caramel complexion.

Alston Louis Duplantier wore big rimmed glasses and his complexion was lighter than mine and Andre's. His jet black hair was cut short. Alston's eyes were lighter, with thinner eyebrows and lips, a small round-shaped face, and a slanted nose. They were dressed up like they were going to church. They didn't look anything like my father. Then I saw why.

Gwendolyn Maria Duplantier was their mother and she came up behind them at the door. Their mother was pale, with brownish green eyes, narrow lips, and high cheekbones. She had perfectly arched eyebrows and a small round nose. Her hair, which she wore in a bun, was long, jet black, and she was very short compared to my mother.

Both of the boys jumped into my father's arms. I thought they were going to knock him down. Ms. Duplantier told them, "Let them in the door."

My father finally introduced me to my brothers and their mother. I curtsied and greeted them. The twins looked at each other in bewilderment.

My father said, "She's my little genius." I had taught myself lessons on etiquette just for the trip. I could see a disgusted look on their mother's face.

This grand home was full of pure class and elegance and had everything. Once you came through the stained-glass double front doors, you were in a marble foyer that led to a grand stairway with an elevator beside it. The house consisted of four floors with seven bedrooms and six bathrooms. The first floor had twelve-foot ceilings, beautiful inlaid pecan floors, custom-designed marble mantles, and a double-sided fireplace. The gourmet kitchen had granite counters with the newest appliances.

The second floor held the master suite. It was a large room with a full bathroom, spacious closet, adjoining library with a fireplace, and a large sitting room spanning a full fifty feet from the rear courtyard balcony to the thirty-foot balcony over the pool. The third and fourth floors each had three-bedroom suites with full bathrooms. Each bathroom had a soaking tub and a walk-in shower.

Ms. Duplantier escorted Papa and me by the elevator to our rooms on the fourth floor. She slept on the first floor in the master suite and the boys stayed on the third floor. My father and I each had our own bedroom and bathroom. Ms. Duplantier announced, "Dinner is at six o'clock." She spoke very properly and asked us to "please dress for dinner."

I sat on my father's bed while he unpacked. It didn't take him long since he only had one suitcase. My mother had three and I had two. My father commented that we were "typical females," whatever that meant.

"In my wildest dreams, I couldn't imagine a house like this." Then I asked Papa, "Why did Ms. Duplantier act like that?"

"Act like what?"

I began to imitate her with hand gestures. "Does she ever smile?"

He laughed. "That's how rich people act, Ray."

"Well, I don't ever want to be rich if I'm going to act like that."

Where we had dinner was called the grand room. There was a large chandelier and colorful flowers on the table for centerpieces. All of the silver was perfectly polished, and the tablecloth was cleaned and pressed. There was a delicious smell from the kitchen that drifted through the mansion. We had food that I had never eaten before.

Our first course for dinner was *turtle soup au sherry*. The second course was a pecan pear salad. I really enjoyed the salad. The main course was a pomegranate molasses grilled rack of lamb, grilled marinated redfish, and grilled asparagus with hollandaise sauce. Aunt Lottie fries lamb chops and bakes her fish. I spit my asparagus in my napkin.

For dessert, we had white chocolate bread pudding. I didn't like that either. Ms. Duplantier noticed the disgusting look I had on my face. She commented that my palate probably wasn't used to this type of cuisine.

During dinner, I listened to Andre talk nonstop to my father. I learned that my brothers had been writing to my father ever since they learned to read and write. He asked him about the train trip because they had never been out of New Orleans.

My father suggested for them to visit us in Washington, D.C. Andre got so excited and looked at his mother and started begging her to let them go. Ms. Duplantier said, "I will give it some consideration." I tried to get in the conversation, but I was ignored. I could see I had nothing in common with him except that we had the same father. My brothers didn't look like him at all. They looked and acted just like Ms. Duplantier.

Children are natural followers. They imitate the traits of their parents whether good or bad. We didn't even have the same last name. They had their mother's last name because their parents were never married.

It seemed that I couldn't stop staring at Ms. Duplantier. There was not a hair out of place and her makeup was applied perfectly. Even her clothes fit her like a model. I also caught Ms. Duplantier and my father staring at each other. My father continually commented on how Ms. Duplantier looked. I made several comments that he was married.

I daydream sometimes when I'm not comfortable with my reality. As I sat at the dinner table, I imagined Ms. Duplantier was my evil stepmother. Andre and Alston were my evil stepbrothers. (I didn't know at the time that was the truth.)

The mansion was an old, drafty castle that I had to clean every day. I snapped out of my daydream when I heard Alston stutter. He had been quiet up until that moment. I made the mistake of laughing. Andre snapped at me and called me a name. Immediately, my father told me to apologize. I saw a look of disgust on Ms. Duplantier's face again. I did not understand why this woman didn't like me. She didn't even know me. No one had told Andre to apologize to me for calling me a name.

After dinner, I happened to be walking behind the twins and their mother as they went up the stairs. She told the twins, "That little know it all and her mother have stolen everything that is rightfully yours."

"What is that, mother?" The twins asked.

"Your father's love," she answered. "I should be married to your father and I am going to get him back." She had delusions that my father still had feelings for her after all these years.

"Alston and Andre, you must put Daddy's little genius in her place. You do whatever you need to crush Raynelle's little heart."

"We will do anything to please you mother," they replied.

How can you feel so threatened by an eight-year-old girl? Unloved and unwanted children often become delinquents of society.

The next day, Andre and Alston woke me by playing loudly with my father. We all got dressed and had breakfast in the same huge room as last night. Breakfast was a lot simpler. We had fresh fruit, multigrain toast, and hot smoked salmon benedict. After breakfast, my father asked Ms. Duplantier if he could take them outside in the backyard.

"I guess so," she answered. I started to follow them.

"No, Ray. Stay inside and get to know Ms. Duplantier."

I said very softly, "I don't think she likes me."

"Who wouldn't like a pretty face like yours?" Was his reply as they went into the backyard.

Ms. Duplantier put on a classical album on an antique turntable and sat down in a big chair. I sat on the couch.

"I have never seen one of those," I told her as I pointed to the turntable.

"Yes, it's been in my family for a long time."

"You really have a beautiful house," I said, trying to make conversation.

"Thank you," she replied.

"How old is it?"

"The Duplantier mansion has been in my family since 1863. The Duplantier name is French for someone who lived by a plantation of trees. We can trace our ancestors back to Canada, New Zealand, and England. The Duplantiers started as slave owners, using the slaves to pick the cotton. Then my great, great grandfather served on the board for the first bank in New Orleans. He later opened his own bank. My grandfather was the first one in the family to start in politics."

Ms. Duplantier went on and on about her family history. I tuned her out every other sentence. I only could hear *blah, blah, blah*. I was jealous because I wanted to be in the backyard playing with Papa and my brothers. I was trying to convince myself that there was no reason to be jealous. I had my father every day and my brothers were only his pen pals.

"I think you are very beautiful," I told her.

"Thank you," she replied.

"Yes, I was thinking that you look like one of those fashion models."

"I would never demean myself and be a fashion model," she replied.

"No, you just look like one," I corrected her. "I feel the same way about my mother."

"Oh really?" She sneered.

"Yes, you two have a lot in common."

"I can't imagine having anything in common with your mother."

I just went on. "She dresses beautifully like you too. My mother has every hair in place and her makeup is just right."

Ms. Duplantier tried to sound polite by stating, "Your mother sounds like she takes a lot of pride in how she looks."

The whole time we were talking, she was looking out at the backyard. A few times while they were playing, she yelled at my father, "Don't be too rough with them."

Children have the right to guidance from their parents. Parents should tell them what to do but also show them the way by a good example. She also reminded the boys, "Not too rough. You're not wearing your play clothes."

Ms. Duplantier slowly turned, looked at me and said, "Raynelle, please tell me a little about yourself. Do you go to school?"

"Yes, I will be starting third grade in the fall."

"You seem very mature to be only eight years old," she replied.

"I hear that a lot. I will be nine in June. I sound older because I love to read." I asked, "Do you love to read?"

"No," she replied. "I prefer to listen to audiobooks on my cassette player when I'm exercising."

"See? That's another thing my mother likes to do." I compared them again, saying, "She often listens to her portable radio while running through the park near our house. Sometimes, I ride my bike with her while she runs."

"I see. I'm sure you miss your mother."

"Yes, she decided to stay with my aunt. I know you already know this because I saw you and my brothers looking out the window."

"Well, your father and mother were making so much noise. I wasn't sure if I needed to call the police or not." I could tell that she didn't like my mother by the way she spoke about her.

I didn't know what she was fishing for during our conversation. After our talk, I got the feeling that Ms. Duplantier hated me more. I saw more disgust whenever I mentioned my mother. After my father and brothers finished playing, it was suggested to the boys that they take me around to show me the area. I could see that it was the last thing they wanted to do.

Andre whined, "Why can't we show you around too father?"

"Your mother and I have to take care of some final plans for your party," Papa's replied. That changed their mood.

As we left the house, Ms. Duplantier reminded them about their conversation the night before. Andre and Alston started treating me better once their mother spoke to them. They showed me their school and their favorite place to play. We played on the playground for a few hours.

"We have one last place to show you," Andre said. "You want to see where our father used to work?"

"Yes, I would like that," I said. We rode a streetcar down to the French Quarter. They took me inside an old abandoned warehouse on the docks. All I could smell was rotten fish. Then Andre threw me down and they both grabbed an arm to hold me down. Out of the dark came two other boys.

The biggest one pulled my dress up and tore my underwear off. I started screaming. The big boy yelled at Alston to shut me up. He saw an old dirty rag and shoved it in my mouth. I could taste fish and dirt. I thought I was going to throw up. Then I felt this terrible pain between my legs. He was so heavy on top of me. I could hardly breathe. Then he got up and the other one got on top of me. He was not as heavy but he smelled like rotten garbage.

I could not daydream to escape this. The pain from my brothers holding my arms down while this grimy and smelly boy laid on top of me kept me from thinking of anything else. I just laid there in the dark and cried bitter tears. I was hoping it would be over soon. I just wanted my Papa. Oh, where was he? I thought hours had gone by, but, in truth, it was only a few minutes.

Andre demanded his money and the two boys paid him. There was one broken window where they were standing and I could see what the boys looked like. I couldn't see how much money Andre collected, but I knew that it could never be enough for what they had done to me. The other two boys quickly left.

Andre came over to me and whispered in my ear, "Now you are a tramp just like your mother."

I started crying again. With a nasty look on his face, Alston said, "You better not tell anyone what happened." Because of his stuttering, it took him forever to say it.

As I got up from the floor, I could barely walk. I felt nauseous and spewed my breakfast onto Alston's shoes. He cursed and then slapped me. My anger rose and I scratched his face.

Andre punched me hard in my arm. Each one took an arm and dragged me to the door. We were about to catch the streetcar back to the house when I saw my mother in a car with a man that wasn't my father. I tried to call her but the man was driving too fast. I didn't know at that time, but it would be the last time I would see my mother for five years.

The boys snuck me through the back door and told me to go get cleaned up. I went to the bathroom and took a bath as hot as I could stand it. I sunk into the tub until my whole body was underwater. I longed to be at home in my own bathtub. I wanted to see my papa.

I don't know how long I was in the tub because I fell asleep from crying. Papa woke me up by knocking on the door.

"Ray, you are going to turn into mush staying in that tub so long. Can I come in?"

"No, I'll be out soon," I replied. I slowly got out of the tub and dried myself off. I put on my pajamas and went into my room. My father was sitting on the bed. I had forgotten about the dirty dress lying on the bed but he didn't see it.

"Did you have a good time with your brothers?" He asked. I wanted to tell him what had happened but I was too scared.

"No, I fell and hurt myself."

"Let me see!"

"No, Papa, I just want to go to bed."

"Ray, let me check you over."

"I'm fine, Papa, I'll be better tomorrow."

"What about something to eat?" He asked with a serious look of concern on his face.

Forcing a smile on my face I told him, "I'm not hungry."

"Okay, Ray, I'll check on you later."

"Papa, have you heard from momma? I thought I saw her when I was out."

"Yes," he said. "She called and checked on you while you were out."

First betrayed by my brothers and now my father had lied to me. How much more can I take today?

My father did come back and checked on me, but I pretended that I was asleep. He came over and kissed me on the cheek and forehead. I just laid there in the dark, wishing I was back home in my own bed. After he left, I locked the door. I did not trust those monster twins.

The next day was Friday, which was the day before the big birthday party. My father tried to come in to check on me.

"Ray, why is this door locked?"

I got up and let him in. It was my turn to lie.

"I thought I heard a noise in the hallway last night. I didn't want to bother you so I locked the door."

"Are you sure you are just eight years old? You act like an old woman." I felt like an old woman after yesterday.

"Are you feeling better today?"

I lied again. "A little."

"Good. Please get dressed. I borrowed one of Ms. Duplantier's cars and I want to take you to meet the rest of our family."

Chapter 1 : A Life Full of Betrayals

I thought to myself, *I don't want to meet anyone else—ever. What excuse can I give him?*

"Papa, I just want to see momma."

He started stuttering. I had never heard my father stutter before.

"I'll take you to see your mother later."

"I really don't want to go anywhere else," I told him.

"Raynelle, you haven't met your Aunt Rebecca and your cousins."

"I don't want to meet them, I just want momma."

"Okay, I'll give them some excuse why you are not with me. So I'll see you when I get back."

"Are you leaving me here?"

"Well, you don't want to go with me."

"Are my brothers going too?"

"No," he said. "They have an appointment to get their picture taken. Ms. Duplantier says it is a tradition every year before their birthday."

"Okay, I'll get dress and go with you."

I didn't want to be away from him again after what those monster twins did yesterday. This also would be the first time to see the place where he had lived when he was just a little boy. Papa mentioned we had to make one stop before driving to Baton Rouge.

"Where?" I asked him.

"We are going to the cemetery where Uncle James is buried."

After we left the cemetery it was approximately an hour's drive to Aunt Rebecca's house. Aunt Rebecca lived with her husband, Earl Foster, and their two girls, Alfrieda and Georgia, in the Audubon University District of New Orleans. Uncle Earl owned a construction company that specialized in renovating old homes. I later found out his company renovated the Duplantier mansion.

Their house was so different from the Duplantier mansion. Their house was built in 1911. It was one of the first homes in this area. It was two stories with four bedrooms, two bathrooms, and it still had the original front doors and hardware. The living and dining rooms had color-accented beamed ceilings. There was a playroom, porch, patio, eat-in kitchen, and a large backyard.

Aunt Rebecca was different from Aunt Debra. She looked and acted more like Aunt Lottie. I was glad that I had changed my mind. Aunt Rebecca had cooked all of my favorite foods. We had beignets (French doughnuts), po'boys (French bread sandwich with seafood inside), seafood gumbo, catfish, and crawfish etouffee (shellfish over rice). It was a feast!

My cousins, Alfrieda and Georgia were so much nicer than my brothers.

"Can I stay here until we leave on Sunday?" I asked Papa.

"No, but you will see them again at the birthday party." I had forgotten all about the birthday party.

The next day, I took my time getting to the backyard for the party. I hated the fact that those two monster twins would get a party after what they had done to me. I was grateful Alfrieda and Georgia were there. I stayed with them during the party.

I saw Andre and Alston staring at me. Then the two boys from the warehouse showed up. All four kept leering at me, whispering and laughing. I started feeling sick. I wanted to go find Papa. Then he came out of the house with Ms. Duplantier holding a birthday cake and singing, "Happy Birthday." I wanted to throw the whole cake right in the monsters' faces.

Alfrieda and Georgia were the last ones to leave. I was so sad to see them leave. I went into the house to go to my room and pack. I was glad that we were leaving this terrible place in the morning. Andre and Alston were waiting for me in my room.

"Get out!" I started yelling.

"What do you mean get out?" Alston replied. "You are in our house."

"Well, you can have your old house!" I shouted at him. "I'm leaving in the morning."

Then Andre spoke up. "Little sister, you can't leave without giving us a birthday present."

"The only gifts I want to give you are two fat lips and to tell Papa what you did to me."

"Now that's not nice." Alston stuttered. Then they both came closer to me.

"If you don't leave me alone, I will yell for Papa right now," I announced.

Then Andre said very convincingly, "We'll leave, but we will be back tonight after everybody is asleep. We will get our present from you!" They both left with smiles on their faces.

I was so scared. Later, my father came in and saw I was packed already.

"Well, I see you are ready to go."

"Yes," I said. "Can we leave now?"

"No Ray, our train leaves tomorrow morning."

After he tucked me in bed, I locked the door again and put my suitcases in front of the door. I was ready for them just in case they got in my room.

My father had once given me a Leatherman because he saw I was intrigued by it and he had no need for it anymore. He told me when I got older he would show me how to properly use it. My mother didn't approve, but I was so glad that I had it tonight.

I had brought the Leatherman as a gift for my brothers. Once I saw the house when we arrived, I decided that the gift was too little. I started thinking about Aunt Lottie and the times we spent together reading the Bible. There were so many characters that defeated their enemies in the Bible. Aunt Lottie said, "God is everywhere." So was He there in the warehouse?

Chapter 1 : A Life Full of Betrayals

I had memorized Psalm 27 for a lesson in my Sunday school class. I wished I had remembered at the warehouse. I started reciting it as a prayer as I waited for the monster twins.

> The Lord is my light and my salvation; whom will I fear? The Lord is the strength of my life; of whom will I be afraid? When the wicked came against me to eat my flesh - my enemies and my foes - they stumbled and fell. Though an army should encamp against me, my heart will not fear; though war should rise against me, in this will I be confident. One thing I have asked from the Lord, that I will seek after – for me to dwell in the house of the Lord all the days of my life, to see the beauty of the Lord, and to inquire in His temple. For in the time of trouble He will hide me in His pavilion; in the shelter of His tabernacle He will hide me; He will set me up on a rock. Now my head will be lifted up above my enemies encircling me; therefore I will offer sacrifices of joy in His tabernacle; I will sing, yes, sing praises to the Lord. Hear, O Lord, when I cry with my voice! Be gracious to me and answer me. When You said, 'Seek My face,' my heart said to You, 'Your face, Lord, I will seek.' Do not hide Your face far from me; do not thrust Your servant away in anger; You have been my help. Do not leave me nor for- sake me, O God of my salvation. If my father and mother forsake me, then the Lord will take me in. Teach me Your ways, O Lord, and lead me in an upright path, because of my enemies. Do not deliver me to the will of my enemies; for false witnesses have risen against me, and they breathe out violence. I believe I will see the goodness of the Lord in the land of the living. Wait on the Lord; be strong, and may your heart be stout; wait on the Lord. Amen.
> -Psalm 27

As soon as I said, "Amen," suddenly there was a noise. Andre and Alston were trying to get in my room and one of them had tripped over my suitcases. I kept still until I felt a hand on me.

Quickly, I pushed the covers back. With all the strength of my eight-year-old body, I stuck the Leatherman deep into Alston's arm. He made the worse scream that I have ever heard.

Papa came running into the room first. He found Alston on the floor. He was crying, kicking, and holding his arm. Andre was yelling and pointing at me, "She tried to kill my brother!"

Papa demanded, "Why are you in her room?"

The little brat yelled at Papa, "This is my house I can be wherever I want."

I heard Ms. Duplantier get off the elevator and run into the room. She could see by the hall light the blood around Alston. She squealed at my father, "We need to get Alston to the hospital."

Papa picked Alston up from the floor and took him to the bathroom down the hall. Alston's cut wasn't that deep. My father had a first aid kit in his suitcase and he bandaged his arm.

They all left me alone there in the dark. I felt like I was three years old again. However, this time I was scared and happy at the same time. I had never really prayed to God. I thanked him for the knife so I could retaliate for what the monster twins had done to me. At first, I thought it was a strange gift for a little girl. I was grateful now. After that day, I have prayed Psalm 27 many more times throughout my life.

Chapter 1 : A Life Full of Betrayals

Papa came back into the room and cut on the light. He closed the door, walked over to the bed, and gently picked me up into his arms. I started crying uncontrollably.

Once I calmed down, he lifted my face and asked, "What was that all about?" I told him everything.

Papa put me back under the covers and kissed my cheek and forehead. As he left the room, I saw that he had taken his belt off.

I heard hollering between Papa and Ms. Duplantier. They were talking so fast I could only understand part of their argument.

Ms. Duplantier cried out, "I don't know why you came back here after all these years!"

"I came back because the boys asked me to and your father was dead. How could you raise our sons to be so cruel? Children are a gift and not puppets to manipulate. You've turned out just like your father."

"I'm nothing like my father!"

"You are everything like your father!" He told her. "I would never believe you would act the very way that you despised about your father."

She cried, "I loved you, and you left me."

"I left because your father threatened to put me in jail for raping you. Remember, I wanted to marry you," Papa said. "I wasn't good enough in your father's eyes."

"You didn't love me! You only asked me to marry you because I was pregnant."

"It was the right thing to do."

"No, the right thing would have been for you to stay."

"Stay and go to jail?"

"My father wouldn't have put you in jail."

"His two bodyguards showed otherwise. It's amazing you are still so naïve. Your father was a powerful man. It was going to be his way only." Ms. Duplantier was surprised about what he had told her.

Then I heard Andre crying. Children have to be properly disciplined and corrected. They need to know that there are serious consequences for their wrong behavior. My father was whipping him with his belt. I felt very good about that. I heard Ms. Duplantier say something about calling the police.

 "The first time I left was because of your father. This time is because of you and your evil sons," I heard my father say, and a door slam immediately after.

Papa came back into my room and told me, "Get dress because Uncle Earl is on his way to pick us up."

Papa and I waited on the front porch of the mansion. I fell asleep on my father's lap.

Everyone was quiet during the ride. It was serenity being held securely in my father's arms. A child has the right to grow up within the security of a loving home and know that they are special. Papa promised me, "I will protect you from this day forward."

When we arrived at Aunt Rebecca's home, she hugged and kissed me for a long time. I felt some comfort from her since my mother wasn't there to do so.

Aunt Rebecca put me to bed with Alfrieda who was my age. I lay in the bed tossing and turning. I couldn't sleep because I was repeating the past two days in my mind over and over. Finally, I got out the bed to ask for some milk. I heard Papa and Aunt Rebecca talking about what had happened to me.

Aunt Rebecca demanded, "You should take her to a doctor for an examination."

Papa said, "I will when we get back home."

Aunt Rebecca asked, "Ms. Duplantier really was going to call the police on you after what her sons did to Raynelle?"

"Sis, you know her family. The Duplantiers with all their money have the police in their back pocket. Mr. Duplantier is dead but things still haven't changed.

Gwendolyn cackled, "She didn't even want us here. It was the boys that kept begging her to invite us. She even had the nerve to accuse me of stalking her. All I wanted to do was to help her plan the party."

Aunt Rebecca had talked with Ms. Duplantier during the months that Uncle Earl and his company were renovating the mansion. She told my father, "Gwendolyn just told him those things because she wanted to hurt him. Gwendolyn's father had disowned her. He only kept her around to watch over his grandsons. She was very empty inside after you left. Gwendolyn never stopped loving you. Losing you turned her into a very bitter woman."

"She knew who the boys were who hurt Raynelle. I have something to confess, Joseph, that I haven't told anyone including Earl. I normally don't like keeping secrets from him."

"What's that?" My father asked.

"I have kept this secret because nobody would have believed me."

"You really have my curiosity in alarm. Please tell me what it is," my father pleaded.

"For Earl's construction business, I work as bookkeeper and secretary. One day, Earl went to work and forgot to sign time-sensitive paperwork that needed to be filed before he started the next construction job. I had no choice but to drive to the Duplantier mansion for his signature on the paperwork.

The servant escorted me into the sitting room where Gwendolyn was just getting ready to have lunch. She invited me to sit down.

Earl was not there and she told me, "You can wait with me until he returns." Gwen was cordial and asked me, "Is there anything I could get you?"

"My response was no. As Gwen was eating, she asked me questions about you. I noticed that she was silently crying. I asked her, *Are you alright?*"

"Gwen said, *Today was my father's birthday*. Gwendolyn started telling me how her father treated her terribly after the boys were born and how she looked like her mother but having children out of wedlock by a Creole shrimp farmer was a disgrace to the memory of her. She was a saint. He accused Gwen of tarnishing the Duplantier family name. The only good thing that he felt came from the mess was his two grandsons and he was going to model them into his image. Her father boasted that the boys would be his legacy."

"Gwen explained that she couldn't let that happen. She seduced one of her father's bodyguards because her father treated him badly and because he blamed him for letting her get pregnant. She said they both were in limbo and had a bond. The bodyguard made a poisonous concoction and she baked it in a French apple tart, which was her father's special dessert that he had before bed every night."

"Gwen said with disgust she had to learn how to bake this dessert because her mother used to fix it for him. There was no proof or evidence of the poisoning. Her father was declared dead by natural causes. He died at his desk one night. I asked her why she was telling me all this. She told me that it was heavy on her heart and that, after this renovation is complete, she probably would never see me again. Gwendolyn even pointed out that no one would ever believe me if I tried to tell anyone."

My father said, "Well, it turns out Gwen was more like her father than he thought."

Aunt Rebecca continued, "I had forgotten about that day until the birthday party. Gwen was looking at me very suspiciously. I believe this is the reason why she was so mean to Raynelle. Ray reminds her of the life she could have had with you."

"The renovations of the mansion and the poisoning started the year you and Lauretta got married. Before that, Gwen had a delusion that you would return to New Orleans to rescue her and the boys."

My father moaned, "This entire evening was like reliving the past. The same three common factors: sex, a threat, and scurry to run away. However, this time it was worse because it involved my sweet and innocent Ray. I am so thankful I wasn't allowed to marry Gwen. It's so hard to comprehend that someone could be so hateful towards an eight-year-old child."

"I don't see how you can say that Gwen still loved me, Rebecca. Well, I can really pick women, can't I? I'm sure Uncle James is shaking his head and saying, *Boy, I told you to stay away from loose women*. Even Lauretta didn't have the courage to tell me herself that she was staying in New Orleans. She had to send a message by Debra."

I went back to bed thinking how I wanted this day to be over. We had to get up early the next morning because Uncle Earl was driving us to the train station. I felt a little better now my father knew everything and we were going home. My thoughts were interrupted when my father walked into my cousin's room.

"Ray," he said, "It will be just the two of us taking the train today."

"Why? Where is Momma?"

"Your mother has decided to stay in New Orleans and get a job," he said.

"What about me?" I asked, feeling very confused. "She doesn't love me anymore?"

"Ray, I don't know what to tell you, all I know is that you have experienced a whole lot of grown-up stuff this week. I'm so sorry."

"Did you tell momma what happened?" I asked.

"Yes. She wanted me to tell you how sorry she was."

It was a very sad day. Aunt Rebecca, Alfrieda, Georgia, and I were crying because Papa and I were going back home. I told them, "I can write." My cousins said, "We'll write back."

On the train ride back home, Papa and I sat across from each other. I could tell my father was in deep thought. I snapped him out of it by sitting on his lap and hugging his neck.

"Papa, I love you."

"I love you too, Ray." We sat in silence again.

I had stated previously that Aunt Lottie was the second most influential person in my life, but my Papa was the first. Later, I asked my father to tell me about his childhood.

He couldn't remember much before he went to live with Uncle James. My father was born Joseph Otis Young in Baton Rouge, Louisiana. When he was four years old, his parents were killed in a plane crash. My Aunt Debra is five years older than my father and Aunt Rebecca is two years older. My father went to live with Uncle James in New Orleans, who didn't have any children.

Uncle James wanted someone to eventually take over his shrimp farming business. He was married once but was divorced because his wife ran off with his business partner. My father's sisters went to live with Uncle Claude and Aunt Charlotte and, for this reason, he didn't see his sisters much while growing up.

They lived in Baton Rouge, which is the capitol of Louisiana. Three times a year—Easter, Thanksgiving, and Christmas—Uncle James would take my father by boat to visit them. Uncle James said Baton Rouge was too big for him and there were just too many loose women living there.

As my father grew older, it was getting harder for him to remember some important things about his parents. He had only one picture of his parents, his sisters, and himself together. Uncle James loved my father as if he was his biological son. He always encouraged him to enjoy the best of life. Uncle James would remind him that life was just a short visit—do not hurry or worry.

Papa didn't like school that much—he mostly got C's. I think his attitude about school came from Uncle James. Uncle James didn't finish high school. He believed that all a man needed in life was to know how to make an honest living. My father did a lot of work for Uncle James before and after school. He didn't take much time to do his homework.

My father is tall at six feet and two inches. He has a caramel complexion with thick brown hair and eyes. The shrimp business helped him develop a muscular build like that of a great athlete and he could have played any sport. My father was a very attractive young man and could have his pick of any young girl that he wanted—many wanted him. Again, Uncle James shot that idea down. My father had no real social life until he turned twenty-one. Uncle James didn't want any woman to treat my father the same way his wife treated him.

My father also enjoyed listening to music. Uncle James couldn't afford music lessons for him so he taught himself how to play the trumpet by ear. My father had saved up some money and bought a trumpet from a Goodwill store. During my father's last year of high school, Uncle James allowed him to get a part-time job at a club playing in a band. The only way Uncle James agreed to let my father play at the club was that it must not interfere with his work. So without fail, my father would get up early most mornings and do his chores. There would also be a lot to do when he got home from school, yet he got all of his work done.

I fell asleep while he was talking.

Biblical Characters for Chapter One

"For I know the plans that I have for you, says the Lord, plans for peace and not for evil, to give you a future and a Hope."
	-Jeremiah 29:11

Raynelle, Esther, and Tamar

Raynelle had Hope in her parents to provide safety and security. The Bible gives the account of two women who had similar life events as Raynelle with Esther (in Esther 1:19-21; 2:2–18; 3:1–12; chapters 4, 5, 7, 8, and 9) and Tamar (in 2 Samuel 13).

Raynelle and Esther have life events that are similar in the fact that both their lives were uprooted from the culture, customs, and family that they were familiar with. Raynelle's parents were unaware of the calculated tragedy that occurred, but Esther's uncle Mordecai was.

Once Joseph found out about the evil Raynelle's brothers did, he disciplined them. Nevertheless, the damage was done to her emotionally, spiritually, and physically.

In the Bible, Tamar shared a similar experience with Raynelle. Tamar was instructed by her father, King David, to care for her half-brother, Amnon. She had no reason to suspect Amnon had evil intentions toward her. Raynelle and Tamar were both betrayed by family members, which caused much pain in their adult lives.

All three of these women had to have Hope in God and God alone.

Chapter 1 : A Life Full of Betrayals

The Story of Esther

Esther was a Jewish girl named Hadassah (the Hebrew word for Myrtle). Orphaned when she was very young, she had been adopted by her cousin, Mordecai. He was a devout Jew from Jerusalem who lived in exile in Susa.

Esther was among the beautiful young women brought to King Ahasuerus by a royal decree to replace the former queen. He delighted with her—as was all of the royal court—and she was crowned his queen. Esther was charged by Mordecai not to disclose to anyone that she was a Jew.

Mordecai was a surrogate father to Esther and she showed him the respect that scripture teaches a child should show to a parent. Even after her move to the palace, Mordecai continued to keep a custodial eye on Esther and advised her to keep her Jewish identity hidden.

Angered by Mordecai's refusal to prostrate himself as it was against Jewish custom, Haman, an adviser to King Ahasuerus, plotted the destruction of not just Mordecai but of the entire Jewish population. Haman, after receiving written permission from King Ahasuerus to destroy the Jewish population, had the royal decrees delivered throughout the provinces.

Mordecai implored Esther to go to the king and plead for her people. It was against the law and dangerous for her to approach the king unbidden, but because of the circumstances, she courageously agreed, declaring, "If I perish, I perish." This was a conscious trusting herself into God's hands. Whatever happened, God would be with her.

Queen Esther fasted for three days, dressed in regal robes, and then approached King Ahasuerus. He received her and Esther cleverly invited the king and Haman to dinner. After the meal, she invited them to a second banquet the following day. Haman was pleased with this newfound royal attention, but his high spirits gave way to anger when he came across his enemy, Mordecai, at the palace gate.

After returning home from the banquet, Haman expressed his contempt for Mordecai to his wife and friends. They suggested that he have gallows fifty cubits tall be constructed and, in the morning, ask the king if Mordecai could be hanged on it. This suggestion pleased Haman so he had the gallows constructed.

When Haman and the king were brought to Esther for the second banquet, she revealed her Jewish identity and told the king about Haman's plot to exterminate her people. Overcome with rage toward Haman, the king rushed out of the room.

Haman, desperate for his life, violated harem law when he threw himself down on the couch beside the queen. Worse, the king found the frightened Haman like this when he returned to the room and ordered him to be hanged that very day on the gallows he had built for Mordecai.

King Ahasuerus gave Queen Esther Haman's estate and appointed Mordecai chief minister in Haman's place. Esther once again approached the king, this time concerning Haman's edict against the Jews. She begged the king to cancel it. The king refused because Persian law made a formal edict irrevocable, even by the king himself. Instead, Ahasuerus gave Mordecai the authority to send out another decree neutralizing the first one by providing new instructions. Now Jews would be given the right to bear arms in self-defense.

On the day Haman had appointed for their annihilation, Esther's people turned on their enemies and wiped them out, including the ten sons of Haman. On the following day, after the killing and mayhem, the Jewish people celebrated not only their survival but their amazing and complete victory.

Later, Mordecai and Esther sent letters to all of the Hebrews, establishing that the Feast of Purim should be commemorated each year on the 14th day of Adar to mark their deliverance from Haman and their enemies.

The Book of Esther is unique to all the books of the Bible. The Book of Esther is the only book of scriptures that contains absolutely no mention of God. This seems very strange, making it almost a *godless* book. It's filled with godlessness, evil people, and evil plans to annihilate the people of God. It's not just the name of God that's missing but, also, it seems, His Presence is missing. Darkness reigns and God is nowhere to be found.

Does this make the Book of Esther less holy than the other books in the Bible? Not at all, it's as holy as all of the other books that mention His name. Even though the name of God is not mentioned, the hand of God lies behind every event. He is there, unseen, unmentioned, yet working all things together and turning every event around to fulfill His purpose.

The Book of Esther is called the Book of the Unmentioned God. Esther speaks of all of the times the presence of God is not felt. His voice is not heard. His hand is not seen. There's no sign of His love or purpose. There are times He seems far away or not there at all.

When all you see is darkness but know His presence, that is the time of the Book of the Unmentioned God. Even though His presence is not felt, He is there. Even though His hand is not seen, He is moving. Even when His voice is not heard, He is speaking, especially in the silence. Even when you feel abandoned and alone, His love is still there. You realize that when He seems hopelessly far away from you, He is still right there beside you, working every detail in your life for His purposes and your redemption. In the end, the light will break the darkness, the good will prevail, and you will know that you were never alone.

The Book of Esther shows how God has kept this promise at every stage of history. Just as Haman met his death by execution, we can trust God to protect us from the enemy, Satan, and to work out His ultimate purpose of redemption in our lives. A careful reading of the Book of Esther will reveal that the book has a spiritual base. The book also teaches a valuable lesson about the sovereignty of God. Although the enemies of the Covenant people may triumph for a season, He holds the key to ultimate victory.

The Story of Tamar

Tamar was the lovely daughter of King David and sister of Absalom. One day, King David sent Tamar to care for her half-brother, Amnon because he lied and said he was sick. Tamar was raped by Amnon.

The passion Amnon had for Tamar was transformed into hatred, for he saw her as the cause of his own moral failure. Rather than take responsibility for his actions, Amnon acted as though Tamar had been the responsible party. He transformed the guilt he felt into hatred of Tamar. She fled to Absalom, who plotted revenge against Amnon.

However, Absalom also advised Tamar to hold her peace and not to take this thing to heart, showing how little Absalom understood how devastating the rape was to Tamar. Rape is not something any woman can or should simply shrug off. Rape is a violation that must be reported and dealt with if the victim is to find any sense of closure or to recover her self-respect. However innocent a woman may be, the emotional damage is severe and must be dealt with.

Absalom was not thinking of his sister's welfare but of how he might take revenge on Amnon. It served Absalom's purpose to have Tamar remain silent, but it did not serve Tamar's needs. Two years later, Absalom got his revenge for Tamar by arranging Amnon's murder.

Another telling comment in the biblical text is, "When King David heard of all these things, he was very angry." What the text does not report is any action on David's part to right the wrong. He did not punish Amnon. He did not rebuke him. He did not follow the law and force Amnon to marry Tamar. David did nothing.

While we cannot excuse it, both as a king and as a father, David was responsible to deal with his son's actions. David's failure to act left Tamar to suffer in silence and ultimately led to Amnon's murder.

What happened to Tamar is a tragic reminder that, sometimes, dreadful things happen to godly people. At times, those we look to for help harm us instead. Only God's healing, mercy, and grace can restore our sense of self-worth and provide a fresh beginning.

> "Don't envy sinners, but always respect the Lord. Then you will have Hope for the future, and your wishes will come true."
> -Proverbs 23:17–18

Lauretta and Leah

Lauretta Ann (Rowell) Young had Hope in herself that she could change Joseph. The Bible gives the account of Leah (in Genesis 29–31) who had similar life events as Lauretta.

Lauretta and Leah both were married to men that were unloving and self-centered. Lauretta had married for the wrong reasons—she had become pregnant and didn't want the same life as her youngest sister.

Leah was forced into marriage by her father and the custom of the day. They both thought they could change their husbands by their actions. Lauretta constantly nagged Joseph to the point that it affected everyone around them. Lauretta was ambitious and wanted more than the life Joseph had given her.

Leah only knew that, by the custom of that day, men were considered blessed by the number of their offspring. Leah continued to have children to try to win her husband, Jacob's love. Eventually, Lauretta and Leah, after much leaning to their own understanding, learned that unconditional love and Hope are found in God alone.

Chapter 1 : A Life Full of Betrayals

The Story of Leah

Leah was the older of two sisters, both married to Jacob. The two sisters grew up in a family of shepherds.

As is sometimes the case, one daughter was beautiful and the other unattractive. The biblical text says Leah's eyes were delicate, which is better translated as weak. Her sister, Rachel, was loved while Leah was ignored.

It remains clear that Rachel was far more attractive than her sister. When Jacob first met Rachel in the fields, taking care of her father Laban's sheep, he fell deeply in love with her. Laban offered to employ Jacob and asked him to name his wages. Jacob offered to serve Laban for seven years for the privilege of marrying Rachel. Jacob had no money to offer Laban for his bride as custom required, so Jacob offered himself and his services.

However, when the seven years were complete, Laban substituted Leah for her sister Rachel. After their wedding, Jacob awoke to discover that the woman he had laid with the night before was not the woman he loved. So, Laban offered to make a second deal for Jacob to earn Rachel by serving another seven years.

Leah's life reminds us that people are overly impressed by appearance. Sometimes, it seems that God alone seems to care about what He sees in the heart. From Leah, we learn to keep our focus on God. Later, we learn that while God had opened Leah's womb as a consolation for being unloved by her husband, Rachel remained barren.

Leah kept looking for love, approval, and acceptance from Jacob, but she was continually disappointed until she reoriented her life toward God. We see this in the names she gave her sons. When the first son was born, Leah named him Reuben, meaning *a son*. Leah believed Jacob would love her now. However, Jacob did not.

When a second son was born, she called him Simeon, meaning *heard*. Despite Leah's gift of children to her husband, she continued to experience rejection.

When a third son was born, Leah called him Levi, meaning *attached*. She believed, this time, Jacob would become attached to her because she had borne him three sons. Again, she was disappointed.

With the birth of her fourth son, Leah began to look away from her husband for love and to look to the Lord. She named her fourth son Judah, meaning *praise*. There is clear evidence that this change in attitude persisted.

After Jacob had had two sons for Rachel by her maid Bilhah, Leah, still in competition with Rachel, insisted he have sons for her by her maid, Zilpah. The two sons Zilpah bore were named Gad and Asher. Leah bore two more sons, Issachar and Zebulun, then finally a daughter, Dinah, meaning *justice*.

We can see in Leah's life experiences that God blesses each of us in different ways. We need to praise Him for the gifts He gives us and not mourn for what we do not have. Leah was the less favored of the two wives of Jacob and she must have been painfully conscious of this during all of the years of her marriage.

However, it was Leah rather than Rachel who gave birth to Judah, through whose line Jesus the Messiah was eventually born.

> "So are the paths of all who forget God; and the hypocrite's Hope will perish, whose confidence will be cut off, and whose trust will be a spider's web."
> -Job 8:13–14

Joseph, Hosea, and Samson

Joseph had his Hope of being able to judge character better than Uncle James. Joseph also held Hope that he had a second chance for a family when he married Lauretta. The Bible gives the account of two men who had similar life events as Joseph.

Hosea is found in the Book of Hosea 1:1-8 and chapter 3, while we learn about Samson in Judges 14–16.

From Chapter 1, we learn Joseph was doomed from the start with his relationship with Gwendolyn. Joseph wanted to marry Gwendolyn out of obligation because she was pregnant, but social differences made this impossible. Hosea was instructed by God to marry his wife, Gomer. Gomer was unfaithful consistently throughout their marriage.

Joseph's history repeated itself by impregnating another woman, Lauretta, before marriage. But, this time, Joseph was able to have a marriage of obligation and not love.

Lauretta, like Gomer, had lovers outside her marriage. Both Joseph and Samson chose women for their physical needs. Joseph's and Samson's sexual desires led to relationships that did not last because their Hope was in themselves.

The Story of Hosea

Hosea was an Israelite prophet who was told by God to marry a prostitute named Gomer. He offered her his love, but she continued to sell herself to any man with money. Gomer finally left her children and husband for her lovers.

When God told Hosea to bring Gomer home, he found her ill, broken, and a slave. Hosea bought Gomer from her lover and took her back home. Hosea loved Gomer again as his wife.

The tone and contents of the Bible also show Hosea was a man of deep compassion, strong loyalty, and commitment to God and His will. He was a sensitive and compassionate spokesman for righteousness. Hosea's own life echoed the message that God is love. Through his marriage and prophetic message, Hosea presents a vivid picture of the steadfast love of God for His people.

The Story of Samson

Samson broke every rule of his Jewish heritage. Despite his rebelliousness, Samson proved an effective—if unwitting—tool of God.

Samson's choices in women caused his downfall and his death. His parents urged him to find an Israelite wife, but Samson would not listen. It's hard for parents to watch their children make disastrous choices in selecting a spouse. We can offer advice and pray, but we cannot choose for them. Often, we will need grace to live with things we cannot change and have faith in God who works all things for our good.

Samson's mighty physical feats are well known, but he was a foolish man. Samson's life was marred by his weakness for women. One of the women he fell in love with was Delilah, a woman who lived in the Valley of Sorek.

When the impulsive Samson took the Philistine Delilah as his lover, he shared with her the secret of his superhuman strength—his unshaven hair. The Philistines had bribed her to find out the key to his strength. So, she teased him until he revealed that his uncut hair was allowed to grow long in accordance with the Nazirite law.

While Samson slept, Delilah called the Philistines to cut his hair and turned him over to his enemies. Samson became weak, not only because his hair had been cut, but because the Lord had departed from him.

After his enslavement by the Philistines, Samson was blinded and forced to work at grinding grain. Eventually, he came to his senses and realized that God had given him his great strength to serve the Lord and his people. After a prayer to God for strength, he killed his enemies by pulling down the pillars of the temple of Dagon. That one great act of faith cost Samson his life, but it won for him a place among the heroes of faith. Out of weakness, he was made strong by the power of the Lord.

Samson was a person with great potential who fell short because of his sin and disobedience. Although mighty in physical strength, he was weak in resisting temptation. His life was a clear warning against the dangers of self-indulgence and lack of discipline.

> "When a wicked man dies, his expectation will perish,
> And the Hope of the unjust perishes." -Proverbs 11:7

Gwendolyn, Delilah, and Herodias

Gwendolyn's Hope was in Joseph and her father's bodyguard to help her escape from her father. Gwen also had Hope in her ability to manipulate her sons to do whatever she wanted.

The Bible gives the account of two women who had similar life events as Gwendolyn—Delilah (in Judges 16:4–20) and Herodias (in Matthew 14:3–11; Mark 6:17–28; and Luke 3:19– 20). Gwen's Hope in a total stranger, Joseph, was so misguided. Gwen had been sheltered her entire life so she couldn't discern lust from love. Joseph tried to explain this to her, but she only saw him as an escape from her controlling father.

Gwen's scorn to get back at Joseph was to use her sons. Herodias used her daughter for revenge on an innocent man of God. Herodias didn't care that the man of God was just pointing out her wrong. He was giving her a chance to repent and get right with God. Gwen, Delilah, and Herodias were only looking for what they could get out of their relationships.

The Story of Delilah

Delilah was a calculating woman. In the midst of turmoil between the Israelites and the Philistines, Israel's judge and mighty warrior, Samson, fell in love with Delilah who was a Philistine. The Philistine rulers lured Delilah with a large reward of silver to find out the secret of Samson's strength and then to betray him.

Delilah was aware of the power her sexuality gave her and was quick to use sex for personal gain. While Samson had fallen in love with her, Delilah only pretended to have affection for him.

She was more than willing to let Samson use her body because she was using him to become rich.

How Samson failed to see what was happening cannot be imagined. Her repeated efforts to get him to betray the secret of his strength seem so transparent. Unfortunately, Samson was blinded by his passion and was manipulated easily. Her pretended doubt of his love and her appeal to prove his love by revealing his secret finally wore Samson down.

Delilah was determined to get ahead and she chose to use sex to advance herself. In so doing, Delilah betrayed not only her lover but also herself. Sex is a gift from God given to bind a married couple together in an ever-deepening commitment. When a man or woman engages in sex outside of that context, especially in a calculated way, he or she is as much a victim as the sexual partner.

Delilah hounded Samson for the secret of his strength. If someone hounds us to do or say something we know we shouldn't, it's time to make it adamantly clear that the issue is not negotiable. The other person needs to drop it or risk the loss of the relationship.

Delilah reminds us that the weakness of the flesh can topple even the most powerful person. Keeping ourselves sexually pure and equally yoked protects us from people like Delilah and is vital for empowering God's people.

In her attempts to trick Samson, Delilah was outwitted three times. First, Samson told her to bind him with seven bowstrings, then with a new rope, and finally to weave his hair with a spinning wheel. When none of these worked, Delilah pestered Samson until he was tired to death and revealed that his uncut hair was the secret of his strength. Delilah had Samson's hair cut as he slept on her lap and gave him to the Philistines, who gouged his eyes out and brought him in triumph to Gaza.

When people choose to have sex outside of marriage, they lose sight of the value God places on individuals. Our culture glorifies illicit sex. As a result, people are becoming desensitized to the evils of sexual impurity. Sexual immorality is a type of slavery. People who use others for their own gratification have no concern for the consequences to others or themselves.

The Story of Herodias

Herodias was a self-centered woman. She abandoned her first husband, Philip, for his brother, Herod. She knew this was condemned in God's law. John the Baptist had strongly condemned Herod for this illicit relationship, earning Herodias' hatred. Her pride and hatred generated a murderous intent. Herodias's response to godly counsel was to retaliate against the counselor. Her anger led her to a far greater sin, as she conspired to end John's life. If we harden our hearts, we make ourselves vulnerable to greater sins.

Herod had John imprisoned, but he was afraid to execute the popular prophet. Herod feared John himself, knowing that he was a just and holy man. Herodias, however, was incensed that John had publicly condemned her. She held it against him and wanted to have him killed. Her chance came when Herodias's daughter, Salome, danced seductively at a feast Herod gave and the king told the young woman to name her reward. When she looked to her mother for advice, Herodias told her to ask for John the Baptist's head. She did not hesitate for a moment to involve her daughter in what was nothing less than the murder of a godly man. Harsh, brittle, and hardened, Herodias cared for nothing but revenge.

> "Hope deferred makes the heart sick, but when the desire comes, it is a tree of life."
> -Proverbs 13:12

Andre, Alston, Salome, and Amnon

Andre and Alston Duplantier used Hope to obtain guidance and parental approval from their mother. The Bible gives the account of two Biblical characters who had similar life events as Andre and Alston with Salome (in Matthew 14:6–11 and Mark 6:22–28) and Amnon (in 2 Samuel 13).

The mothers of Andre, Alston, and Salome did not show any concern for the character development of their children. By using them in their evil schemes it gave the approval that revenge is acceptable. The consequences of revenge caused mental pain, physical pain, and death. Amnon wasn't given evil advice by a parent but it was still a family member who had a significant influence on his life. Amnon's choice to take the advice eventually led to his death.

The Story of Salome

Salome's mother, Herodias, left her father, Philip, and married Herod, her uncle. Since this marriage was forbidden by law, John the Baptist openly criticized Herod and Herodias, for which he was arrested. Herodias wanted him killed for his comments against her, but Herod refused to execute him.

Salome danced before Herod at his birthday party, pleasing him and his guests so much that he agreed to grant her whatever she wished. After conferring with her mother, Salome asked for John the Baptist's head on a platter. Regretfully, the king fulfilled his promise by having John beheaded and presenting the head to Salome, who in turn gave it to her mother.

The Story of Amnon

Amnon was the son of King David and a half-brother of the beautiful Tamar, who was his sole consuming interest. Amnon raped his half-sister, which ultimately brought hatred and strife to the whole family. The passion Amnon had had for Tamar was transformed into hatred because he saw her as the cause of his own moral failure.

Rather than take responsibility for his actions, Amnon acted as though Tamar had been the responsible party. He transformed the guilt he felt into hatred for Tamar. Amnon had acted against what he knew was right. No person can violate deeply held personal convictions without drastically affecting himself as well as others.

As the eldest son and crown prince, Amnon was in line to inherit the throne of David. Before he could assume any royal office, his half-brother Absalom avenged Tamar's rape and abuse by murdering Amnon.

Chapter 1 : A Life Full of Betrayals

Chapter 2

Unexpected Destiny

Uncle Claude and Aunt Lottie picked us up from Union Station. Aunt Lottie grabbed me and bear-hugged me as Aunt Debra had. I had never felt any real maternal feelings from Aunt Lottie until we returned from New Orleans.

Aunt Lottie started paying closer attention to me. My experiences had caused me to change in various ways. I didn't like any smells that reminded me of the warehouse and couldn't watch any show that had a rape or attack scene against women.

Aunt Lottie noticed that I had started biting my fingernails. She introduced me to fingernail polish. Polishing my fingers kept them out of my mouth because they looked so pretty. Aunt Lottie also began to cook my favorite dish, shrimp jambalaya, every other Sunday after church. Traditionally, she had only cooked it on special days like my birthday.

Aunt Lottie reminded my father, "She needs a physical and counseling. She has gone through two traumatic events from the rape and her mother's abandonment. There is a couple at my church who are child psychiatrists."

My father said, "No, I am not going to risk having her taken away by strangers."

"Raynelle needs the physical anyway for school," Aunt Lottie explained to him.

Aunt Lottie murmured, "I hope it is not the money that's making you reluctant to get Ray some medical care?"

My father agreed to take me to get a physical. He explained to me, "You need one for school." When we came back from the doctor's office, my father told Aunt Lottie everything physically checked out okay.

Aunt Lottie grunted, "It's a miracle she's fine physically but her spirit was crushed by her mother and brothers."

The following Sunday after church, Aunt Lottie gave my father a pamphlet from the child psychiatrists at her church. He was suspicious about what Aunt Lottie discussed with them.

Aunt Lottie told him, "I only mentioned that my niece's mother had abandoned her. I decided not to tell them about the rape because they would not understand why the police didn't get involved."

Reluctantly, my father promised to read the pamphlet. The pamphlet started explaining the need for therapy. My father became intrigued and continued to read.

Therapy can help kids develop problem-solving skills and also teach them the value of seeking help. Therapists can help kids and families cope with stress and a variety of emotional and behavioral issues. Other kids need help to discuss their feelings about family issues, particularly if there's a major transition, such as a divorce, move, or serious illness.

Significant life events such as the death of a family member or friend, divorce or a move, abuse, trauma, abandonment by a parent, or a major illness in the family can cause stress that might lead to problems with behavior, mood, sleep, appetite, and academic or social functioning. In some cases, it's not as clear what caused a child to suddenly seem withdrawn, worried, stressed, or tearful. However, if you feel your child might have an emotional or behavioral problem or needs help coping with a difficult life event, trust your instincts.

Consider a number of factors when searching for the right therapist for your child. What are his or her credentials? A good first step is to ask if the therapist is willing to meet with you for a brief consultation before you commit to regular visits. Not all therapists can do this given their busy schedules and some charge a fee for a brief consultation while others consider it a free visit.

When your child expresses emotional issues, be there to listen, care, and offer support without judgment. Patience is critical too, as many young children are unable to verbalize their fears and emotions. Try to set aside some time to discuss your child's worries or concerns. To minimize distractions, turn off the TV and don't answer the phone. By recognizing problems and seeking professional help early on, you can help your child and your entire family move through tough times to happier, healthier times ahead.

After reading the pamphlet, my father decided to make us an appointment that Friday to meet the child psychiatrists, Dr. Madeline and Dr. Jerome Thomas. I didn't want to go meet these psychiatrists, but I wanted to please Papa. The first thing we had to do was fill out a questionnaire. It was a lot of questions. Their secretary took the questionnaire from my father and then we waited another fifteen minutes before actually seeing the two doctors.

Dr. Madeline introduced them both to us. She tried to have a conversation with me by repeating the questions from the questionnaire. I would reply with one-word answers; I really didn't want to talk at all. Dr. Jerome did the note-taking.

After forty-five minutes, an alarm went off and the secretary came to get me so the doctors could talk to my father only. They explained to him, "She is depressed and we recommend giving her a prescription for it."

My father asked, "Did you determine that just from a questionnaire and meeting us one time? I could have told you she was depressed. I brought her to see you for a solution."

They tried to explain their credentials and ten years' experience entitled them to be able to diagnosis depression.

"I'm not putting my eight-year daughter on any drugs!" My father called them quacks and said, "You should be ashamed of yourselves."

"Your anger is not necessary," Dr. Jerome told my father. He suggested that my father try another type of therapy from the pamphlet and offered a referral to another doctor.

The last thing my father said when he left their office was, "Between Aunt Lottie, Uncle Claude, and me, we'll figure this out." He grabbed my hand, and we left the doctor's office. Papa apologized to me for putting me through this. I reassured him, telling him it was okay, but it wasn't okay. It took me about a year before I started acting like my old self.

My father was glad that Aunt Lottie was out of town so he wouldn't have to answer all of her questions about how the appointment went. He was still angry and he didn't want to take his anger out on Aunt Lottie for suggesting that we see the doctors.

Aunt Lottie had gone on an overnight trip with the church choir to New York to see a play. After the store closed that night, there was a thunderstorm and I couldn't sleep. At least three times a week I couldn't sleep all night. My father was a sound sleeper, so I would slip into his bed beside him.

I went to my father's room to get in his bed, but he wasn't there. I remembered that Uncle Claude was staying with us for the night because he didn't want to be alone. I heard Uncle Claude and my father talking in the kitchen. My father was explaining the reason why he came to Washington, D.C.

Uncle Claude is usually quiet and reserved. He usually said Aunt Lottie did enough talking for the both of them. I guess since she wasn't around Uncle Claude was able to get some words in.

My father explained that Uncle James talked a lot also and gave me advice while growing up. He said he followed most of his advice until the summer after his twenty-first birthday. This was the year he started playing at the House of Jazz. Uncle James continually reminded my father, *Son, those girls down at that club are nothing but trouble. Don't ever fall for any girl who would throw herself at you. Look for a good girl with integrity and self-respect who will allow you to pursue her.* My father continued telling Uncle Claude about his first encounter with Ms. Duplantier.

The second year after Papa started playing at the House of Jazz, Gwendolyn Duplantier walked into the club. Gwendolyn was educated at a boarding school and had been sheltered from a lot of things. For her high school graduation present, she had begged her father to let her stay a week in New Orleans unsupervised. Her father, Charles Louis Duplantier, was a very powerful city council member. Therese Jackson, who was Gwendolyn's best friend, went along with her on this trip.

Even though they were underage, they were able to buy fake IDs without their parents knowing. They wanted to go out to a club and the minimum age to get in was twenty. They asked one of the hotel's staff the name of the best club in the French Quarter. He told them it was the House of Jazz.

When they stepped into the House of Jazz, they were very impressed when a bouncer took them to a table near the front. They were laughing and talking until the band started playing. The music took them into another world—one that they had never experienced before. Gwendolyn could not take her eyes off the trumpet player.

Gwendolyn and Therese left just before the club closed. Later that night when Gwendolyn tried to sleep, she knew in her heart that she had to get to know the trumpet player. With great anticipation, Therese and her went back the next night. She asked the waitress what the trumpet player's name was. "That's Joseph Young," she replied. Gwendolyn kept repeating his name over and over under her breath.

After the first music set, Gwendolyn watched as Joseph Young went to the bar. Boldly, Gwendolyn slipped into a stool beside him. He glanced at her from the corner of his eye. Immediately the words of Uncle James about *loose girls* started ringing in his ears.

Gwendolyn started the conversation by introducing herself and asking about the band, how long he had been playing, and who had taught him to play so well. She was impressed when he told her that he was self-taught.

Gwendolyn said, "You look more like a Joe than Joseph. Can I call you Joe?"

"Sure, why not." Then my father asked Gwendolyn her age. She lied and said twenty. He knew better.

"No, you are about eighteen," he told her.

"No, I'm twenty," and she took out her fake ID.

"Sweetie, I know the person who made this fake ID for you. Do you see that symbol in the corner? Well, that's his signature mark."

Gwendolyn felt so stupid. He sensed that she was uncomfortable.

"He gets everybody," my father told her.

"When you show the fake ID, flash it real fast like this." He demonstrated to her how to do it. Papa changed the subject.

"Gwendolyn is a long name. Why don't I call you Gwen?"

"So, Joe, you don't mind talking to me?" she asked.

"No, because all we are doing is just talking."

They kept talking until the next music set. He shared about Uncle James' shrimp farming business and that he wants him to take over one day.

"My passion is to become a professional trumpeter and singer."

"I'm an only child. My mother died before they could have more children. I have attended girls boarding schools for as long I can remember."

"One day, I overheard my father say that he didn't want me around because I reminded him too much of my mother. My father is a very powerful man, but my mother was one of the few persons who wasn't intimidated by him. From what I heard, my mother brought out the best in him."

"After my mother died, he became a cold, unfeeling, and unloving person. I discovered a letter about the doctor in charge of her mother's care. The letter stated that this doctor contributed to my mother becoming addicted to pain medicines. My father was going to use this information to get revenge for my mother's death."

Gwen and Therese again left before the club closed. They had no idea that someone had been watching them for the past three days and nights—one of Gwen's father's bodyguards. He came up to Papa as he was placing his trumpet in its case.

"Hey, kid, do you know who you were talking to tonight?" He asked with a firm voice.

"Yes, I think she said her name was Gwen."

"Her name is Gwen; Gwendolyn Duplantier. Her father is Councilman Charles Duplantier."

"Is that supposed to mean something to me?"

"Yea, it means to stay away from her or there will be trouble for you," was his firm reply.

"Mister, I don't want any trouble, all we were doing was talking."

"Well don't even talk to her!" The bodyguard gave his warning as he left the club.

The next night, Gwen and Therese revisited the club. It was my father's night off. Therese had tried teasing Gwen by saying, "Your lover boy isn't here tonight. Can we go somewhere else, please?" Therese asked her.

"No, I'm not feeling so good. Let's go back to the room."

"Gwen, you sure have taken the fun out of this trip."

When my father came back to work, he avoided Gwen all night. Gwen didn't understand it. She thought that they had got along just fine.

Gwen decided that they would leave the club early that night. She decided to sneak out and go back to the club and follow him to where he lived. By this time, she had recognized her father's bodyguard.

When Gwen saw Papa leave the club, she followed from a distance in the shadows. It seemed that he was walking for miles and she lost him when he turned into a dark alley. Gwen didn't know exactly where he went and then she saw a guy standing by a wall smoking.

"Sir, have you seen a tall guy carrying a trumpet case come by here?"

Chapter 2 : Unexpected Destiny

The guy said, "No, but I'm available." He grabbed her and started rubbing his hands all over her.

Gwen started yelling when, suddenly, Papa came up behind the guy and knocked him out with his trumpet case. He grabbed Gwendolyn's hand and they went running down the street.

My father took her inside his house. Uncle James had turned one of his boathouses into a private place to live. He made Gwen some tea to calm her down because she was shaking.

"Is there someone I can call to come and get you?" He asked her.

"No," she replied. "If my father finds out about this, he will never let me out of his sight again."

"Gwen please tell me why you followed me home?"

"I thought we were getting to know each other," She said. "Then tonight you completely ignored me. I wanted to find out why."

"Gwen we come from two different worlds," He told her. "I'm three years older than you, Gwen. All we can ever be is friends." Gwen had other plans.

Papa didn't tell her about the warning her father's bodyguard had given him. He gave her a shirt and told her that she could sleep in his bed and he would sleep on the couch. However, during the night, Gwen came into the living room, knelt by the couch, and began to kiss him.

At first, he pushed her away, but she wouldn't stop. He started kissing her back and then they both gave in to their lustful feelings.

The next morning, my father took Gwen back to her hotel. Feeling guilty and ashamed, he told her, "Last night was a mistake. I take full responsibility and I'm deeply sorry for taking advantage of the situation."

"You didn't take advantage of me. I love you."

"Gwen this isn't real love but lust."

Gwen started crying and ran upstairs to her hotel room. She cut the trip short and went back home.

A month later she found out that she was pregnant. She was so scared about what her father would say and do when he found out. Gwendolyn phoned my father at the club to tell him that she was pregnant. He told her not to worry and that he would work things out.

For days, Uncle James could see that something was on papa's mind. He finally inquired, "Son, you can't get ulcers from what you eat, but you can get them from what's eating you."

It was hard, but Papa told Uncle James about Gwendolyn.

"Joseph, I raised you to be an honorable and decent man. I think you know what the honorable and right thing to do is."

Uncle James explained, "Although I have taught you to always take responsibility for your actions, this is the one time that it is not going to work. Mr. Duplantier is not going to let his daughter marry you, no matter what."

"Uncle James, you're wrong."

Chapter 2 : Unexpected Destiny

"Joseph I've been on this earth a lot longer than you. I've lived in this city all my life. I know what I'm talking about."

Later that day, my father called Gwen back and told her what Uncle James had said. She made up in her mind that she loved him even more.

The day came when my father was to meet Councilman Charles Duplantier and he wore his best suit and tie. He had pawned his trumpet to buy an engagement ring.

Needless to say, Papa was very nervous as he walked into Councilman Duplantier's office. He noticed the bodyguard who had threatened him standing far off in the corner with a mean look on his face. Even though Uncle James had given him a lot of wisdom, it was not enough to prepare him for this meeting.

Papa was naïve to the fact that, in New Orleans, there were two kinds of people: the *haves* and the *have nots*. Councilman Duplantier definitely was in the category of the *haves*. Uncle James and Papa were the *have nots*. Two entirely different social groups.

When my father started working at the club, Uncle James told him the Young family history because there had been a lot of racial tension and he didn't want him to get hurt.

"Everyone is not like the people you grew up with," He said. "People judge you by your social status, race, gender, and any other way you might be different than them."

My father was so naïve when it came to prejudice. He had never encountered it before. It was a whole different world in the shrimp business. Regardless of race or color, everyone respected each other and looked out for one another. It was like an extended family.

The *haves* that came to the club where he played jazz just wanted to have a good time. There were no social divisions. Everyone had the same goal to listen to good jazz music and eat some of the most delicious New Orleans cooking.

With his best smile and holding his hand out to shake, Papa said, "Thank you for meeting with me Councilman Duplantier."

The councilman just ignored his etiquette. "I am a very busy man," was his blunt reply. "What is it that you want Joseph Young?"

Papa was not surprised that this man knew his name. "Sir, I am here to ask for your daughter's hand in marriage."

With a look of unbelief, he replied, "Why would I even consider letting a shrimp farmer marry my daughter?"

Papa felt the sweat begin to roll down his whole body. He looked directly into his face saying, "Councilman Duplantier, sir, I am an honest and hard-working man. My uncle raised me to always take responsibility for my actions."

"And what actions are you taking responsibility for?"

"Sir, Gwendolyn is pregnant with my baby."

Quicker than a bolt of lightning, Councilman Duplantier leapt from his chair, grabbed my father, and started strangling him. The bodyguard pulled him off.

Councilman Duplantier looked at the bodyguard and said, "This is your fault! You're fired, now get out!"

Immediately, Councilman Duplantier called in two other bodyguards. After a few minutes, the councilman calmed down. He looked at Papa with hate in his eyes and with his finger poking in his chest.

"You no good shrimp farmer! You will not marry my daughter! You will not even see my daughter again or the child that she is carrying. These two men will escort you to get your things and you will take the next train out of New Orleans! If you ever try to get in touch with my daughter again, your uncle will have a terrible accident. Do I make myself clear?"

Papa was so afraid that all he could do was nod his head. He didn't really want to leave, but Councilman Duplantier had also threatened to put him in jail for rape. He also told him that he could ruin Uncle James and his shrimp business. My father couldn't let that happen.

The two bodyguards did escort Papa back to his house. They waited outside while he told Uncle James all that happened and he was completely heartbroken. He called Aunt Lottie and Uncle Claude. Both said that Papa was welcomed to come with them and live in Washington, D.C. This was the first time that my father had ever seen Uncle James cry.

They said their goodbyes at the train station. My father left everything that he ever loved behind. He was determined never to let another woman near his heart again.

After Papa left Louisiana, he called every Sunday to check on Uncle James. He found out the bodyguard was demoted to being Councilman Duplantier's groundskeeper. He was not fired only because he had one and two-year-old sons. His wife had died and all he had was his boys. Councilman Duplantier sympathized with the bodyguard because Gwendolyn's mother was dead also.

I later learned that the bodyguard turned groundskeeper's sons were the boys that raped me. Their father had told them to look after the twins and the twins controlled them like puppets. They lived in the guest house behind the Duplantier mansion.

Uncle James died the year that I was born. Many people thought Uncle James was my father's biological dad. We had similar features and even the same mannerisms. Papa didn't go to the funeral because of Councilman Duplantier. He was so disappointed that he couldn't go to the funeral. Uncle Claude told my father that Uncle James died from a broken heart. His shrimp business went bankrupt because he didn't manage things. After my father left, Uncle James didn't have someone around that had his best interest at heart to help him change with the times.

These were the terrible circumstances that took my father to D.C. and away from his family. My father was now away from the shrimp business, his band, and Gwendolyn with their unborn child. However, he started to appreciate the change after a few months. My father said it took a long time to shower each day when he lived in New Orleans to get the fishy smell off of him and even then he would almost bathe in cologne.

Uncle Claude, Aunt Lottie, and I went to church on Sundays. Papa went with us on Mother's Day, Easter, and Christmas so Aunt Lottie called him a C.M.E Christian. I went home with Uncle Claude on Saturday so I could go to church with him and Aunt Lottie. My father had told Uncle Claude that he thought he had a solution to me not staying all night in my bed. He overheard the hardware store owner discuss that he had glow-in-the-dark wallpaper with stars. My father installed the wallpaper on my bedroom's ceiling while I was gone.

After dinner on Sunday, Uncle Claude and Aunt Lottie drove me home. I usually get out of the car by myself and went up to our apartment, but Aunt Lottie got out of the car also and followed me upstairs. This was a shock because Aunt Lottie had arthritis and didn't like to climb stairs. When I opened the door, my father was sitting on the couch watching a football game. I went over and kissed him on the cheek and started walking to my bedroom very slowly.

Aunt Lottie walked over and stood in front of the TV to block my father from watching it. It took him by surprise because he didn't hear her come in. Aunt Lottie very loudly said, "Joseph Otis Young, how could you embarrass me like that?" I knew it wasn't good for Aunt Lottie to say all three of his names together.

My father tried to explain that the psychiatrists suggested that I take medication to get over being depressed. Aunt Lottie replied, "Oh Joseph, did you have to call them quacks?"

"They're lucky that Ray was with me or I would have called them something worse than that. They didn't tell me anything that we didn't already know. I'm glad it was a free consultation because I wouldn't have paid a dime."

Aunt Lottie became more serious and said, "Then it is up to us and the good Lord to help our little Ray. Love covers a multitude of sins." My father knew better than to say anything else when Aunt Lottie started quoting scriptures.

Papa got off the couch and hugged Aunt Lottie. I knew Aunt Lottie couldn't stay mad at him. They started laughing.

My father said, "Let me help you down the steps to your car." Aunt Lottie reminded him about the football game.

My father replied, "My team was losing anyway."

I went to my room to get ready for bed. I still didn't see the stars on the ceiling because it wasn't dark yet. But after I took my bath and went back to my room, I saw them. It was magical.

Papa heard me go back into the room and he stood at the door. "With your active imagination, you can pretend that the stars are your guardian angels looking over you."

I ran to him and kissed and hugged him. We both started crying. "Thank you. I love you so much."

"I love you more."

Papa was right. The stars did make me feel safer and I slept through the night.

The relationship between me and Papa changed. No more constant arguing; things were quieter and calmer. On Saturday nights, Papa played trumpet while I sang. Uncle Claude and Aunt Lottie would dance to our music. They both said, "You should start a father and daughter group."

Papa said that public performances were in his past. Aunt Lottie teased and told me all the time that I had an old soul because of the singers that I like to mimic. I liked Ella Fitzgerald, Betty Carter, and Billie Holliday.

Chapter 2 : Unexpected Destiny

Two of my favorite songs were performed by Louis Armstrong and Ella Fitzgerald, "Summertime" and "Dream A Little Dream of Me." Ella Fitzgerald was known as the First Lady of Song and as Lady Ella. I also imitated "God Bless the Child," "New Orleans," and "When You're Smiling," which were sung by Billie Holliday. Betty Carter sang another song that I liked called "It Don't Mean A Thing (If It Ain't Got That Swing)."

Our routine changed on Sundays. We would have lunch at The Wharf. The Wharf was the only place in Washington, D.C. that reminded my father of home. All of the boatmen knew him. They all invited him to go fishing. He would tell *that's in the past*.

Papa brought Aunt Lottie's grocery list. When we got home, my cooking lessons started. Papa's cooking came in second place to Aunt Lottie's. He drilled in my head the two secrets to Louisiana cooking. First, use the best seasonings. Second, slow cook over a low flame. Papa and Aunt Lottie made their own seasonings fresh. They didn't trust store-bought seasonings.

Aunt Lottie started leaving clues around the family store for me to find little gifts. The treasure hunt was a joint effort between Uncle Claude and Aunt Lottie. Uncle Claude wrote out the clues for the hunt and Aunt Lottie decided the hiding places. Papa would just look at us and laugh hysterically. The treasures were never anything expensive, sometimes candy or costume jewelry, but my favorite was books. She knew how much I took pleasure in reading.

After the very first treasure hunt, she said to me, "The main reason for time is so all of life doesn't happen at once." I didn't fully understand what she meant until I got much older.

Every treasure hunt, the clues seemed to get harder, sometimes taking several hours or days. After finding my treasure, I would always hug her and say, "I love you, Auntie."

She would say, "Kind words are the oil that keeps the friction out of life."

One time, after observing how close Aunt Lottie and I had gotten, Papa said: "Ray, always remember to never underestimate the power of a touch, a smile, a sweet word, a listening ear, an honest compliment, or an act of kindness. Any one of these has the potential to turn a life around." That's what Aunt Lottie had done for me.

I wanted to one day have a husband just like Uncle Claude. A day didn't go by that he didn't show some type of affection. Uncle Claude would give her a kiss on the hand or a hug. Uncle Claude always held the door open for Aunt Lottie. The fact that Aunt Lottie was taller than Uncle Claude didn't make any difference. A few times he kissed her on the back of her neck if she was sitting down. He thought no one saw him. They showed how a husband and wife should love each other. I never saw them argue or heard them raise their voices. At times, I would catch them dancing around the kitchen to jazz music.

Uncle Claude had many offers to start his own medical practice when he retired from the Army. He said, "I had enough of the politics and bureaucracy that went along with that profession." It made a significant impact on him the number of times he had to perform surgery on a young man during Vietnam. It reminded him that any of these young men could have been Andrew, his son, or Joseph, his nephew.

Chapter 2 : Unexpected Destiny

Uncle Claude stated, "I'm content with whatever time I have left on this earth to spend it with my beloved Lottie. She is the joy of my life." Couples at the café always asked, "What is the secret to your lasting marriage?" They said in unison, "Respect for one another and good communication." They also explained that, if they ever had a disagreement, they never went to bed angry and would make a compromise.

The next year, toward the end of May, Papa asked me what I wanted to do for my tenth birthday. I just shrugged my shoulders up and said, "I don't know." He suggested that we invite the new neighbors next door and have a picnic at the zoo. Then he said, "We can come back home and have ice cream and cake."

I said, "Okay, but I'm not that good at making friends."

There was a four-unit apartment building next door to the grocery store. We walked over the next day and introduced ourselves. I let Papa do all the talking. Then we invited them to the party at the zoo.

Mrs. Davis and her girls, Karen and Sharon, were from New York City. Mrs. Davis' husband had abandoned her after Karen was born. My father wanted to tell Mrs. Davis that he understood what she was going through, but he didn't. Karen was my age and Sharon was three years older. I could never participate in any sleepover except at Mrs. Davis' apartment. Mrs. Davis would try to flirt with my father, but he didn't pay any attention to her. However, she did get some attention from him when she volunteered to do my hair every morning before I went to school.

Mrs. Davis was the school's secretary, which meant she had to be at the school early. Papa walked the girls and me to school. Mrs. Davis walked us home.

Of course, Mrs. Davis had no idea what my mother had done to my father. He never dated. Many women who came to the grocery store had tried to get his attention, but he was not interested. I didn't think he would ever fall in love with another woman again. It seemed to me that his main purpose in life was to protect me.

One Sunday, I heard my father whispering on the phone to someone when I came back from church. My mother wanted him to pay for her to come back to D.C. He refused. She told him that she would find another way back and take me away to somewhere that he wouldn't find me. She always knew the right buttons to push with my father. He finally agreed on the terms she wanted for her to stay away from me. She agreed.

When I was fourteen, I was told that Aunt Lottie and Uncle Claude had decided to sell the business. They asked my father if he wanted to buy them out. He said no, that this was their dream. My father told them that he was moving us to the suburbs of Maryland because the neighborhood was changing. Rival gangs were fighting constantly. Uncle Claude and Aunt Lottie were relocating to New Orleans. They would live at Magnolia Estates where Aunt Debra worked. They asked my father if he would do an inventory for the business sale while they were away making their living arrangements. He agreed.

My father began to close the store early every night. I often stayed over at Mrs. Davis' place because he would be late getting home. I still wasn't allowed to stay by myself even though I was fourteen and getting ready to start high school. Karen, Sharon, and I were in their bedroom watching our favorite TV show. Suddenly, there was a loud knock at the door. We were curious, so we went into the hallway to see who was knocking at the door.

It was two policemen. I recognized one of them as Officer Lawrence who came to our school to give a talk on using drugs. He also showed the students some defensive moves if a stranger approached them. Some defensive moves included blowing a whistle, screaming, running, and kick the stranger in a soft area of their body. I still had my Leatherman and that was all I needed.

The policemen asked Mrs. Davis to step outside of the apartment when they saw us in the hallway. As we went back to watch television, we heard the door close. Mrs. Davis came into the bedroom. We could see that she had been crying. She took me by the hand and we went to her bedroom. She closed the door after us. I knew that it could not be good.

I felt my heart start racing fast. She held me in her arms as she told me that Papa had been shot during a robbery at the store. I immediately screamed. Karen and Sharon came running into the room. The three of them just hugged me and we all cried together. I cried myself to sleep that night. I slept with Mrs. Davis in her bed.

The last words that I heard that night were Mrs. Davis telling Karen and Sharon that Uncle Claude and Aunt Lottie were on their way back from New Orleans. Aunt Lottie woke me the next day by her smell. She always smelled like honeysuckles. Uncle Claude drove us to the hospital. As we were riding, Aunt Lottie explained to me that my father was shot in the head. She said, "He will not look like himself. His head is bandaged, he has a lot of machines around him, and there are a lot of tubes all over his body." The ride to the hospital seemed like it took hours.

I didn't know that much about Uncle Claude's Army career. He was highly respected as a neurosurgeon and had written several published articles about gunshot wounds to the head. Uncle Claude had operated several times on soldiers who were shot during war times. Uncle Claude knew some of the doctors on my father's medical team because of his medical background.

He borrowed a model of a brain from one of the doctors and explained my father's injuries to us. Nothing Aunt Lottie said to me could prepare me for what I saw lying in the hospital bed. A nurse was checking on one of his IV's and his hospital gown fell off his shoulder. Then I saw what confirmed that this man was truly my Papa. My Papa had my name tattooed on his chest. He told me it was so I would always be near his heart.

I ran out of the room and bumped into this woman. I was crying so hard I couldn't see and this strange woman just put her arms around me and hugged me tight. I felt like I wasn't really there, that this was all a dream, and that I couldn't wake up. Then Uncle Claude and Aunt Lottie came out of the room looking for me.

"Hi Aunt Lottie and Uncle Claude," this strange woman said. I stepped back.

"Hi Lauretta," Aunt Lottie spoke back to her.

I repeated her name, "Lauretta." With surprise, I then said "Momma."

"Yes, Ray, it's me." I fainted.

Chapter 2 : Unexpected Destiny

When I regained consciousness, I was in the waiting area. My head was on Aunt Lottie's lap with a cold compress on it.

She said, "All this is too much for you at one time." Uncle Claude brought me some water and told me to drink it slowly.

I told them, "I had a dream that my mother was here."

They both looked at each other. Aunt Lottie spoke and said, "It was not a dream. She is in your father's room waiting on us."

Aunt Lottie explained everything to me. My mother had come back from New Orleans after a year and started coming to Aunt Lottie's house. She had known that was the one place my father and I wouldn't be. Aunt Lottie was reluctant to talk to her at first. She felt she was doing it behind my father's back. Aunt Lottie didn't agree with his decision and arrangement not to let my mother have contact with me. Aunt Lottie felt that my mother had a right to know how I was doing.

My mother convinced my father to pay for college so she could become a dentist. She had completed three years prior to marrying my father. My mother only needed five more years to receive her dental degree.

After church, Uncle Claude, Aunt Lottie, and my mother would have dinner. Aunt Lottie would tell my mother what I had been doing. If I had taken school pictures, she brought her one. If I had received an award or certificate, Aunt Lottie would make her a copy of it.

Aunt Lottie told me, "Your mother needed to learn how to love. She had been so self-centered that she didn't care about anyone else. It was God's plan that she started attending the church after her pastor preached a sermon series on love. The pastor explained, 'God created mankind to have a personal relationship with Him and then with each other. God's commandment, not suggestion, is to love Him with all of our soul, mind, and body. Only then we can love one another.'"

When Aunt Lottie and Uncle Claude decided to move, that's when she told my father how much my mother had changed. My mother was an active member of the singles club, sang in the church choir, and volunteered on mission trips. Aunt Lottie insisted that my father contact my mother and write out a detailed letter that if anything happened to him who would take care of me.

I had a mixture of emotions from this information. I felt anger and betrayal because everyone kept this from me. Resentment also came back from her abandoning me five years ago and disgust because she was in my father's room while we were in the waiting room.

When we went back to my father's room, he was still in a critical condition, but the doctors were optimistic about his odds. Before the doctor started to talk, Aunt Lottie motioned him to step outside the room with us. Dr. Herald explained that the bullet that struck him had traveled the length of the left side of his brain. It had entered from the back and exited through the front of his head. My father was responsive to voice commands after the shooting and had been in the operating room within thirty-eight minutes, according to the medical center.

The doctor explained that swelling tissue of the brain can increase after the first forty-eight to seventy-two hours from the gunshot wound as well as surgery. Although it may take weeks or months for the doctors to be able to determine the extent of any permanent damage, the bullet's trajectory was cause for optimism. A person's chances of surviving this type of trauma to the brain depends on the area of the brain that was struck, the velocity of the bullet, and whether the bullet exits the brain.

The weapon used was a Beretta model 92fs 9mm parabellum semi-auto pistol. The previous year, this weapon became the United States military's official sidearm. If a bullet passes through both the right and left hemispheres of the brain instead of being confined to one side—as it was in this case—the damage is likely to be much worse. The brain is somewhat resilient. It can sometimes tolerate losing one half.

Dr. Herald continued to explain that a person whose brain was pierced by a bullet on only one side has a better chance than someone who has suffered an injury to both sides. It's also a positive sign if the bullet misses the brain stem and the thalamus. These deep structures are crucial to consciousness and basic functions such as controlling breathing and the heartbeat. A person also has a better chance of recovering if the bullet misses the major blood vessels that bring oxygen to areas where it's needed.

Dr. Herald told us that the left side of the brain, where my father was struck, controls language, speech, and the movement of the body's right side. The fact that he was responding to those speaking to him after his injury shows that he had a very good sign for his recovery. Dr. Herald wouldn't speculate on lasting damage.

"That's the mystery of brain injury. There's no way to predict just how much disability a wound that passes multiple regions will leave because our neural connections are so individual."

The medical team treating my father had removed part of his skull. That allowed the brain to swell without being compressed inside the skull. The brain is like Jell-O in a jar—Dr. Herald explained that if it doesn't have any place to expand, there can be even more damage. Confinement of the tissue can prevent blood flow. Fortunately, the bullet had stayed on one side of his brain without hitting the brain's center where such wounds almost always prove fatal.

For now, Papa's biggest threat was brain swelling. The bone removed was being preserved and could be reimplanted once the swelling diminished. This was a technique Uncle Claude had used in the military with war injuries.

Swelling often peaks on the third day after such an injury, but, in my father's case, doctors may wait as long as several months to replace the bone. With a gunshot wound, they may be worried that the bullet had brought in bacteria. They want to make sure there's no evidence of infection before they replace the skull.

After this first report, Aunt Lottie called all of the women from her church to start a phone prayer line for my father. She also made it known to his medical team that there would be no medical updates discussed inside my father's room. Aunt Lottie said there would be no negative talking at all around him. Aunt Lottie quoted to me from Proverbs, "A man's stomach will be satisfied with the fruit of his mouth and with the increase of his lips will he be filled. Death and life are in the power of the tongue, and those who love it will eat its fruit." (Proverbs 18:20–21)

Chapter 2 : Unexpected Destiny

She followed that with, "Let no unwholesome word proceed out of your mouth, but only that which is good for building up, that it may give grace to the listeners." (Ephesians 4:29) Aunt Lottie explained to me that Papa's medical team was only depending on their limited abilities, but we as a family were going to depend on God and His Word.

My father was being kept in a medically induced coma, which was deep sedation that rested his brain. It required a ventilator so he couldn't speak. Uncle Claude said it was too soon to know if he could speak if the ventilator was removed.

Doctors periodically lifted his sedation to do tests such as asking him to raise two fingers or squeeze someone's hand. These actions implied a very high level of functioning in the brain. Papa still may need to undergo additional surgery to relieve swelling or remove a blood clot should one develop.

Dr. Herald announced the following week, "The brain remains swollen, but the pressure isn't increasing, which is a good sign for recovery. The swelling in his face has improved tremendously and his kidney functions were normal."

Uncle Claude said, "You get shot in the head, you should be dead. Your father is a fighter and that's why he didn't die. He's been thinking, hearing, and following commands. This is remarkable! So far so good."

There are few statistics, but doctors agree that well over 90% of gunshot wounds to the head are fatal. A study of 600 Maryland cases found that 95% were dead before arriving at the hospital. The pre-surgery outlook is important because doctors can't reverse the bullet's damage, they just remove fragments and do what they can to fight infection and swelling. Luckily, my father's surgeons didn't have to remove a lot of dead brain tissue.

A bullet that crosses into both sides, or hemispheres, of the brain can leave extensive and lasting damage. Sometimes you are left with slurred speech, personality changes, and paralysis that confines a person to a wheelchair. It can take weeks to tell the extent of damage and months of intense rehabilitation to try to spur the brain's capacity to recover.

After the shooting, Uncle Claude and Aunt Lottie didn't move to New Orleans but sold the store. We rarely left Papa's bedside where he remained heavily sedated. Aunt Lottie and I posted healing scriptures on index cards around my father's room. We included:

- Deuteronomy 7:15
- Psalm 103:1–5; 107:19–20; 118:17
- Proverbs 4:20–23
- Isaiah 53:5; 57:19; 58:8
- Jeremiah 30:17
- Matthew 8:13; 8:16–17; 9:35; 18:19
- Mark 5:34; 11:22–24
- Luke 6:19
- John 14:13–14; 15:7; 16:23–24; 16:26–27
- James 5:14–15
- 1 Pet. 2:24
- 1 John 5:14–15
- 3 John 2

We also had inspirational and gospel music playing continuously. One night, as I sat by my father's bed, I started singing the song he wrote for me when I was a baby. I saw his fingers moving!

I ran out of the room and got his nurse. Two weeks later, my father had another surgery, his sedation had been reduced, and he could breathe on his own. Four days later, he opened his eyes. My father's status improved steadily, and he began simple physical therapy, including sitting up with the assistance of hospital staff and moving his legs upon command. Dr. Herald performed a tracheotomy, replacing the ventilator tube with a smaller one inserted through my father's throat to assist independent breathing.

An ophthalmologist surgically repaired my father's damaged eye socket, but he would need additional reconstructive surgery later. My father's condition improved from critical, to serious, and to good. Approximately a month later, he was transferred to a rehabilitation center for a program of physical therapy, occupational therapy, and speech therapy. The medical experts' initial assessment was that my father's recovery could take from several months to more than one year.

Upon his arrival at the rehabilitation center, his doctors were optimistic, saying, "He has great rehabilitation potential." Four months later, Papas' doctors reported that his physical and language production abilities had improved significantly, placing him in the top 5% of patients recovering from similar injuries.

He was walking under supervision. He developed perfect control of his left arm and was able to write with his left hand. He was able to read, understand, and speak in short phrases. With greater effort, he was able to produce more complex sentences. Early in his recovery, he wanted to attend my junior high graduation. Dr. Herald gave his permission for Papa to attend. Aunt Lottie told me that God deserved all of the praise for my father's improvements and that God gave the doctors wisdom. She then read out loud, "Then they cried unto the Lord in their trouble, and He saved them out of their distress. He sent His word and healed them and delivered them from their destruction. Let them praise the Lord for His goodness and for His wonderful works to the people!" (Psalms 107:19–21)

The month after my graduation, my father underwent cranioplasty surgery to replace the part of his skull that had been removed to permit his brain to swell after the gunshot to his head. The surgeons replaced the bone using tiny screws and a piece of molded hard plastic. They expected that his skull would eventually fuse with the plastic. Tragically, during the surgery, my father's brain started bleeding from an infection. He never regained consciousness.

During the funeral, I saw Aunt Debra. I had not seen her since I was eight years old. Deep in my heart, I still blamed her for my mother staying in New Orleans. I met other family members that I had never seen before. I tried my best to be friendly, but, in truth, I just wanted to be alone.

I was angry with myself for all of the times I had yelled at Papa for being overly protective. Often I would tell him, "I'm not eight years old any longer, so stop acting like a mother hen!" Yet I knew deep in my heart that he had felt guilty for what my brothers had done to me. We never talked about it, yet I could tell. When I saw Aunt Rebecca and my cousins, I ran to them. We had stayed in touch over the years.

Chapter 2 : Unexpected Destiny

After the funeral, there was a repast at Uncle Claude and Aunt Lottie's house. I didn't feel like eating anything. I wished that this was all a bad dream and that any minute I would wake up. I knew Aunt Lottie was grieving just as much as I was. A year before my father came to live with them, their beloved son, Andrew, had been killed by a drunk driver. Aunt Lottie was in too much pain to attend the court trial, but Uncle Claude went each day. Once the guilty verdict was announced, Uncle Claude called Aunt Lottie and told her. The following week, she went to the jail to see the man who had killed Andrew. Aunt Lottie said, "For my healing, I had to look into the eyes of the man who killed my Andrew."

During the funeral and, later at the repast, a young man had been staring at me. Then I saw Aunt Lottie go over and talk to him. This young man was my brother Andre! I hadn't seen him in eight years. It surprised me to see that Ms. Duplantier and Alston also came to the funeral. I made sure to stay close to Uncle Claude. I overheard that they were going back to New Orleans right after the repast. I was so glad.

Soon after the last person left, Aunt Lottie and my mother walked over to me. "Hello Raynelle," she said. I didn't say anything. When she sat down beside me, I moved to another chair.

"Raynelle, I know that you are mad at me." I didn't say a word. Aunt Lottie gave me an envelope with my name written on it. I recognized Papa's handwriting. I stared at the envelope for a long time before I opened it.

My dearest Ray,

If you are reading this letter it means that I am no longer with you. I am so sorry Ray! I'm so sorry that I'm not there to keep my promise to always protect you. I'm mostly sorry for keeping your mother from you.

If Aunt Lottie has followed my instructions, your mother should be there with you as you read this letter. Ray, it's not your mother's fault that she hasn't been in your life these past five years. Your mother came back to D.C. a year after we did. She wanted me to take her back and said that she was ready to be the best wife and mother on earth.

Ray, I didn't want to take the chance of her hurting you again. I felt that I couldn't give her the chance to abandon us again.

Your mother had nothing when she came back to Washington. I helped her find a place to stay and also paid her college tuition so she could become a dentist. I did all this as an agreement that she must never try to contact you in any way.

Now that I'm no longer with you, everything must change. Uncle Claude and Aunt Lottie are older now. They have earned the right to start a new life in New Orleans. Always remember, Ray, I will love you forever. Please, Ray, forgive your mother and go live with her.

With tears in my eyes, I kept reading Papa's letter over and over again. I could hear his voice speaking to me from the letter. Somehow, the last sentence stuck most in my mind. *Go live with her.*

Here is déjà vu. By another person's selfish act, I had suffered the consequences. I had lost everything I loved in one moment. My papa, my uncle, my auntie, and now the only place I knew as my home. I didn't want anything more to do with God because Papa died and I had to go live with the woman who had abandoned her only child for another man.

Aunt Lottie saw the expression on my face and took me by the hand into another room. She put her loving arms around me and said, "A lot of things we will go through and we will not understand on this side of Heaven. But God does hear our prayers and healed Papa, but not on this earth." Usually, her words comfort me, but this time she was very far from the mark.

That night I thought about the song Papa wrote for me. I had it on a cassette tape, so I could always play it. I played it every night before I went to bed, especially when we came back from New Orleans. I played it less and less after Papa died because it was too painful. I missed him so much.

Biblical Characters For Chapter Two

"Now faith is the substance of things Hoped for, the evidence of things not seen."
    -Hebrews 11:1

Aunt Lottie And Jochebed

Aunt Charlotte (Lottie) had Hope in God for wisdom and guidance to help Raynelle. Also, Aunt Lottie had Hope that Lauretta would take good care of Ray. The Bible gives the account of Jochebed (in Exodus 2:2–10) who had similar life events as Aunt Lottie.

Aunt Lottie and Jochebed, in different circumstances, had to give up custody of someone they loved. Aunt Lottie had raised many family members and earned the rest for the time she had left on this earth. Joseph and Aunt Lottie had thought of Ray's future before his tragedy happened. Aunt Lottie had demonstrated to Lauretta how to love Ray and have Hope in God to help raise her.

Jochebed did not have the knowledge to plan ahead for her son. The government of her day made these plans instead. Jochebed giving up her son was to save his life. These two women had to have Hope in God and His love for these two children.

The Story of Jochebed

Jochebed was the daughter of Levi and the mother of Aaron, Moses, and Miriam. To protect Moses from Pharaoh's command that every male Hebrew child be killed, she had placed him in an ark of bulrushes onto the river.

Jochebed, like many mothers today, lovingly gave her child up for another to raise. God honored her by using her son for His godly purposes. God used all of Moses' circumstances to make him into the man He needed him to be.

Jochebed's experiences show us that mothers need to be flexible and creative, especially during difficult circumstances. Jochebed stands as a reminder to parents never to lose faith that God will work in the lives of their children. Most parents live to see this, but some, like Jochebed, don't. How wonderful it is to understand that, even after we aren't here to pray for our children, God continues to answer our prayers.

After Pharaoh's daughter discovered the baby, this young woman showed compassion, not on one of her own, but on the child of an enslaved race—a child condemned to die. We must be reminded that every child is precious to God and deserves our compassion.

Jochebed became his nurse. The adoption by a woman with a compassionate heart saved Moses, who was a child slated by God for greatness. Adoption may do the same today. We do not know the plans God may have for a life.

Pharaoh's daughter and Jochebed remind us that, while leaders and the laws of the land may give us the go-ahead on certain behaviors, ultimately, it is God's Law written on our hearts to which we are responsible.

"Remember Your word to Your servant, on which You have caused me to Hope. This is my comfort in my affliction, for Your word revives me."
 -Psalm 119:49–50

Uncle Claude And Abraham

Uncle Claude had Hope in God for directions to make the right decisions for his family. The Bible gives the account of Abraham who had similar life events as Uncle Claude (in Genesis 11:27-31; chapter 13; 14:8–16; 15:2–5; chapters 16 and 17; 18:1–15; 21:1–7; and 22:1–19).

Uncle Claude and Abraham were the patriarchs of their families. Their families depended on the relationship these two men had with God. Uncle Claude was a perfect example of a godly husband, businessman, and friend. His medical background and a praying wife made a significant impact on Joseph's care.

Abraham had a promise from God that he would be the father of many nations. Abraham complete obedience to God made a significant impact on the future Israel nation.

The Story of Abraham

Abram was a man of profound faith and he was highly regarded wherever he went. When Abram was seventy-five years old, God made a dramatic call on his life.

God told Abram to leave Haran for a new land that God would show him. He promised that He would make Abram a great nation and vowed to bless Abram and give him a great name. In answering God's bidding, Abram gave up his pagan beliefs, ties to his people, and his status as a wealthy landowner. Along the way, Abram honored the Lord and the Lord reminded Abram that He would keep his promise to Abram and his descendants.

Walking by faith, however, was no easy task and it not always the choice Abram made. While in Egypt, Abram lied about Sarai, claiming that she was his sister. She was indeed his half-sister, but he didn't want the Egyptians to know that she was also his wife. No doubt the motive for his deception was based on the social laws of that time. (In Egypt, a husband could be killed if someone wanted his wife.) Abram wanted to protect himself, but it almost cost him dearly.

Thinking she was Abram's sister, Pharaoh brought Sarai into his household to add her to his harem. Abram was lavishly compensated for her with servants and livestock, but losing her would have meant that his promised blessings from God could not be realized. Fortunately for Abram, God intervened by sending plagues on the palace. When he discovered the truth about Abram and Sarai, Pharaoh returned Abram's wife to him and gave orders for the Hebrew family to take their belongings and go.

They left Egypt and returned to the hills north of Jerusalem. Soon, however, it became clear that there was not enough room or grazing ground for the large encampments of Abram and his nephew Lot. Abram resolved the problem by agreeing to let Lot move to the fruitful Jordan valley that was part of Abram's Promised Land. Abram and his camp settled in the plain of Mamre near Hebron. Once there, Abram renewed his worship and faith by setting up an altar to the Lord. He not only defeated four notorious kings and established his military prowess, but his triumph was also symbolic of his spiritual strength and faith.

When Abram was ninety-nine and Sarai was ninety, God spoke to him again, giving him the name Abraham and reminding him that he would be the father of many nations. Also, at this time, God changed Sarai's name to Sarah and told Abraham that she would finally give birth to a son. Abraham laughed at this news but was later reminded of this promise by three strangers—angels in disguise—who visited him. Sarah, well past child-bearing age, also laughed when she overheard this announcement, but in time, Isaac was born to them as promised.

Still, there was trouble in Abraham's clan. Some years earlier, the childless Sarah had given her maid to her husband so that their household would have an heir. Hagar, the slave girl, bore Abraham a son called Ishmael. As a result of Ishmael's birth, Hagar threatened to replace Sarah as the mother of Israel.

Bitterness and jealousy grew between Sarah and Hagar over Ishmael and Isaac. Sarah told Abraham to get rid of Hagar and Ishmael. Sarah did not want Ishmael to share Isaac's inheritance. Abraham was troubled by Sarah's request, but the Lord instructed him to do as Sarah asked but also told him that his descendants through Ishmael would be a great nation. Abraham gave Hagar and Ishmael supplies and sent them off.

Abraham's faith was most severely tested when God told him to kill his son Isaac as a sacrificial offering. Obediently, Abraham started toward the land of Moriah on his donkey, taking with him two servants, his son Isaac, and some firewood. On the third day of the journey, they were near the mountain where the sacrifice would take place. Abraham and Isaac walked the rest of the way alone. Isaac questioned his father about the sacrificial lamb. Abraham assured Isaac that God would provide the animal.

When they reached the place, Abraham built an altar, bound Isaac, laid him on the firewood, and took up a knife to kill his son. At the last moment, God intervened by providing a substitute offering. Abraham saw a ram trapped in a bush and the animal was sacrificed instead of the boy.

In this one act, Abraham performed an extreme demonstration of his faith and God indicated that the common pagan practice of child sacrifice would not be tolerated in the Hebrew faith. God then renewed the promise of blessing to Abraham and his numerous descendants. After this, Abraham and Isaac returned to their home in Beersheba. The Lord's promise of descendants as numerous as the stars of the heavens was once again reaffirmed as a result of Abraham's unquestioning obedience.

In the New Testament, Abraham is presented as the supreme model of vital faith and as the prime example of the faith required for the Christian believer. He is viewed as the spiritual father for all who believe in Jesus Christ. If anyone deserves to be called God's friend, it is Abraham.

> "Chasten your son while there is Hope, and let not your soul spare for his crying."
> -Proverbs 19:18

Uncle James and Mordecai

Uncle James had Hope in Joseph making the right choices for the future. The Bible gives the account of Mordecai who had similar life events as Uncle James (in Esther 2:5-7, 10–11, 19–23; chapters 3,4; 5:9-14; chapters 6, 8, and 10).

Uncle James loved Joseph as a biological son. He was transparent to Joseph about his life mistakes and experiences. Uncle James had Hope that his honesty would keep Joseph from making irreversible life mistakes.

Mordecai wanted to save Esther, his adopted daughter, from the culture she married into. Her new surroundings were not friendly to her Jewish heritage.

The Story of Mordecai

Mordecai is best known as the adoptive father of his orphaned cousin, Esther. He raised Esther to have confidence, to respect her Jewish roots, and to remember all that he had done for her. Later, after she was selected to marry King Ahasuerus and became the Queen of Persia. She won the king's favor for her fellow Jews in exile and, with the help of Mordecai, reversed a death sentence against her people.

Mordecai came into conflict with the Persian Prime Minister, Haman, when he refused to bow down before Haman because he felt that such an act would be idolatrous. The vain Haman was outraged and plotted revenge, not just against Mordecai, but his people as well by ordering all Jews in Persia to be killed.

Mordecai reminded Queen Esther that she was in a position to save her people and she successfully did. Their enemy, Haman, was eliminated by his own devices that he purposed for Mordecai. King Ahasuerus gave Queen Esther the house of Haman and she revealed that Mordecai was her adopted father. The king took off his signet ring, which he had taken away from Haman, and gave it to Mordecai.

Mordecai was now second in command to King Ahasuerus. He used his new position to encourage his people to defend themselves against the scheduled massacre planned by Haman. Persian officials also assisted in protecting the Jews, an event that is now celebrated by the annual Feast of Purim.

> "Command those who are rich with things of this world not to be proud. Tell them to Hope in God, not in their uncertain riches. God richly gives us everything to enjoy."
> -1 Timothy 6:17

Charles Duplantier, Ahab, and Haman

For Charles Duplantier, Hope was in his wealth, power, and control over everyone. The Bible gives the account of two men who had similar life events as Charles with Ahab (in 1 Kings 16:29–33; chapters 18, 21; 22:4–40 and 2 Chronicles 18) and Haman (in Esther chapter 3; 4:7–8; 5:3–14; 6:4–14; and chapter 7).

Charles, Ahab, and Haman were men who sought power at anyone's expense. Charles had a small area of control compared to King Ahab and Haman, but their self-serving decisions affected their families and the people they governed. Their power-driven lifestyles led to the downfall and death of all three men.

The Story of Ahab

Ahab was a compelling figure politically. He was clever at foreign policy and an economic genius. Ahab undertook a major renovation of his own capital, Samaria, including adorning the palace with ivory. He was known for his love of wealth and showy extravagance.

Ahab strengthened the friendly relations with Phoenicia that King David had begun when he was king. He sealed the friendship between the two nations with a political marriage to Jezebel, the notorious wicked daughter of Ethbaal, the king of the Sidonians.

False religion soon led to immoral civil acts. Because Jezebel had neither religious scruples nor regard for Hebrew civil laws, she had a man named Naboth tried unjustly and killed so that Ahab could take over his property. Throughout Ahab's reign, the prophet Elijah stood in open opposition to Ahab and the worship of Baal, the pagan god.

Despite his successes in political and military affairs, Ahab went against the mandated religious practices of Israel by allowing and even practicing, paganism. The biblical record states that Ahab did more to displease the Lord than any of the previous kings of Israel.

Ahab was warned by the prophet Micaiah that he would lose his own life during a battle at Ramoth Gilead. Ahab ignored Micaiah's warning and went to Ramoth Gilead. A stray arrow pierced Ahab and, by the day's end, he had died in a pool of his own blood. Ahab was buried in Samaria and his son, Ahaziah, became king.

The Story of Haman

Haman was the prime minister of Persia under King Ahasuerus. When Haman commanded that the entire king's staff bow down before him, Mordecai the Jew refused because he viewed such as an act as idolatry. Haman's anger toward Mordecai turned to hatred of all Jews, whom he then targeted for extermination by royal decree.

Haman's hatred for Jews went beyond one man's snub, but it had its roots in history. Haman's people, the Agagites, and Mordecai's people, the Hebrews, had battled each other for years—always to the death. This age-old war was now being played out through Haman the Agagite and Mordecai the Jew.

Haman plotted to hang Mordecai and then annihilate all Jews. That plan was foiled by Mordecai and Queen Esther. In the end, Mordecai was vindicated and then honored in Haman's place. After his evil intentions were revealed, Haman was executed by the king on the very gallows he had intended for Mordecai, while Mordecai was given Haman's position as prime minister. This shows that God is always in control of events, even when wickedness and evil seem to be winning out.

Chapter 3

Changed Heart

It hurt me for a long time that my mother hadn't left New Orleans to come back with my father and me. What helped me to get over the abandonment was that I had my father all to myself. I was also happy that there was no more intense arguing every day.

About a year after moving in with my mother, I found out the real reason my mother came back to Washington, D.C. The wife of the dentist she was working for in New Orleans had found out about the affair between my mother and her husband. The wife exposed the affair all over town and my mother couldn't get another job.

When Uncle Claude, Aunt Lottie, and I were clearing my father's things out, we discovered a big trunk in the back of his closet. Uncle Claude broke the lock off, opened the trunk, and to our surprise, there were neat piles of money stacked together. I saw every denomination—ones, fives, tens, etc. There was so much money that we all lost count trying to sort it all out. We also found an insurance policy listing me as his beneficiary. This was another part of Uncle James' world philosophy. Don't use banks!

Uncle Claude and Aunt Lottie took me to a bank and opened a savings and college fund account for me. I was going to miss Uncle Claude and Aunt Lottie. We were all scheduled to move at the end of that summer. Uncle Claude and Aunt Lottie would be returning to Louisiana. My new life would be in the upper northwest section of Washington, D.C., with my mother.

My mother had changed back to her maiden name, Rowell, after the divorce. Defiantly, I addressed my mother as Lauretta to antagonize her. I had no respect for her because she had left me in despair during the most crucial time of my life. I told her she could have gone to court to get shared custody. She tried to explain that my father had threatened to take me back to New Orleans if she did.

One day, Aunt Lottie saw how I was treating my mother and the discouraging look on Lauretta's face. She decided desperately to have a talk with my mother. Aunt Lottie started the conversation with one question.

"Don't we all respond better to a person who takes an interest in us and expresses affection than to someone who tries to force or manipulate us to comply with their wishes?"

My mother answered, "We do with an expressed affection and interest."

Aunt Lottie told her, "Ray is no different."

Aunt Lottie reminded her that it had been five years and she didn't know me anymore. She told her, "Practice attentive listening, which entails an eagerness to hear everything with regard to her thoughts, feelings, and experiences. It's more than just keeping your mouth shut. Make full eye contact and don't interrupt or prematurely formulate an answer. Careful listening will encourage Ray to bare her soul to you and share her innermost thoughts and life circumstances."

Aunt Lottie explained to her that she would need to show a lot of patience and not to be anxious for immediate results. She clarified by saying, "You will have to earn Ray's trust and it is not going to be easy."

"Uplifting words give life. Ray should be the constant recipient of your encouragement. This encouragement can come in many forms and for many reasons. Write a note and encourage her in front of someone else. Also, you can point out her personality traits and the unique talents you appreciate. Don't let a day go by without communicating these encouraging thoughts to her."

"Discipline, correction, and training are ineffective when void of tender love. However, these same tools are welcomed more readily if they come with a kind and gentle hand. Make it a point to discover your daughter's hobbies. Talk to her about them, and learn to share in her enthusiasm. You may even go a step further and participate with her in her favorite activities. Taking an interest need not require financial expense, but it does call for a heart of love and enthusiasm for the things your daughter enjoys."

Aunt Lottie recommended showing genuine affection to me from the moment I woke up until I went to bed at night. She explained, "You can do this verbally by simply saying, 'I love you' many times a day. Eventually, you can express physical affection through hugs and kisses."

Aunt Lottie shared that among the ways she expressed tender love to me was to plan special outings and find unique ways to make memories. She also threw in a surprise or two because everybody loves a surprise. Aunt Lottie ended the conversation by telling her, "Just be the kind of warm and affectionate mother Ray wants to spend time with."

Chapter 3 : Changed Heart

Where my mother lived was so different from what I was used to. My mother had a large house. The living room, kitchen, and dining room were on the first floor. My mother had the master bedroom and her office on the second floor. My bedroom was on the third floor, which she had decorated in my favorite color, purple. She told me if I didn't like anything she would change it. I told her everything was fine.

My mother's dental practice was in the back of her house. Although all of her clients were rich, she also did some volunteer work one day a week at a retirement center. Before I came to live with her, she had volunteered on several mission trips to third-world countries. She had some pictures on her office wall. I appreciated the fact that she didn't push herself on me but gave me time to just be comfortable around her.

My mother was never a good cook, so my father had done all of the cooking while they were married. She never liked Louisiana cooking. When we lived together as a family, she ate a lot of salad, fruit, and vegetables. I think she started being a vegetarian then. So it wasn't a surprise that she had a housekeeper. Her name was Shirley Ann Bowman and she was from Halifax, North Carolina. She came to Washington, D.C. to help her sister raise her six children because her husband had died suddenly. Now that all the kids were grown, she felt she needed something to occupy her time.

My mother was the children's dentist—that's how they met. Ms. Bowman didn't live with us but took the bus in the morning and a taxi in the evening. My mother wanted her to catch a taxi both ways, but Ms. Bowman refused. Because my mother was a vegetarian, Ms. Bowman often stated, "This job is a lot easier than my former employers."

My mother didn't have any parties and we ate out on the weekend. There wasn't that much cleaning needed either because my mother spent so much time in her dental office. She even had a separate professional cleaning service for that. I told Ms. Bowman she didn't have to clean my room either.

I was used to cooking and cleaning for my Papa and myself. I didn't plan on becoming a vegetarian, so I cooked for myself. I would prepare gumbo, po'boy sandwiches, or jambalaya—just enough for that week. I also whipped up skillet cornbread or beignets each day. They tasted better fresh and hot. Ms. Bowman was impressed. She often said that my cornbread tasted better than hers. That was saying a lot. Her cooking was just as good as my Aunt Lottie's. My mother's kitchen was very big, so Ms. Bowman and I never got in each other's way.

It was very important to my mother that I attend the Washington National Academy, which is also known as the Academy. This school was approximately an hour's drive from our house. During the summer, she convinced me to attend the open house to learn about the Academy's offerings and the admission process. I was intrigued by the school's curriculum, so I decided to apply.

The Academy was founded by two brothers in 1950 from Oslo, Norway. It was known worldwide because of all the prestigious awards received and from newspaper and TV stories written about it. It is accredited by The Middle State Association of Schools and Colleges. The Academy had been recognized numerous times by the United States Department of Education as a school whose students achieve at high levels. The previous year, the school was ranked number twenty in the nation in the U.S. News and World Report magazine.

The Academy was previously a historic 19th-century school building. An addition had just been completed that built upon and enhanced the school ambiance. The new building included state-of-the-art labs, classrooms, a large commons area, a new computer room, and the school's first controlled observatory. On the third floor was a spacious roof terrace. The entire five-acre site provided a sense of security and the continued creation of a strong learning community.

The Academy's mission is built upon strong moral values. From admissions and alumni outreach to public service and academics, all activities are structured to promote creativity, curiosity, open-mindedness, love of learning, persistence, and an appreciation of excellence. Students are expected to value their independence and recognize the responsibilities associated with thinking and acting independently.

The acceptance to the Academy was a strenuous process. The first step was to submit a completed application to be considered. The first requirement was to have a 3.0 GPA in core subject classes, which wasn't a concern because my GPA was 4.0. The school also requested a copy of my transcript/final report card from the previous school year and two recommendations from the school faculty. All documentation had to be sent by certified mail to the Academy.

I passed all of the requirements and moved on to the next phase. I had to take a standard written test which included multiple-choice math (Algebra I and Geometry), multiple-choice reading comprehension as well as write an essay.

Students had as long as they needed to complete the tests. The tests were scored based on the highest score of the students tested. Therefore, the school could not tell the exact score the students would need to be admitted to the next phase. I scored a ninety-six on the test.

A decorative envelope came in the mail with an invitation for my mother and me to appear for the panel interview. The invitation stated that the Academy encouraged students and parents to do their best by being themselves. All students must bring their attendance records from the current school year from August through February. My mother had to contact the hospital where my father was hospitalized to acquire medical documents to explain my absence during the time he was there.

The panel consisted of three members of the school's faculty and three senior students. I was extremely nervous because I didn't know what to expect. My first question was to explain my reason for wanting to attend the Academy. That one was a cinch. The next four questions were more personal. What were my views on capital punishment, drugs, war, and finally, what was my religious preference? I felt like I was running for president instead of applying for a school acceptance. Students are admitted based on both their admissions test performance and their interview.

The admissions results were delivered by certified mail. I asked my mother to open the letter. After reading the letter, she gazed at me with a joyful look and announced that I had been admitted to The Academy! I think my mother was more excited than I was because she was crying.

The orientation for all new students was in July. Although it was just a few weeks before school was to start, my mother had not bought me any clothes. She said that we could go shopping together.

Chapter 3 : Changed Heart

I wasn't used to buying new clothes. Aunt Lottie and I went shopping at consignment stores. Even though the clothes weren't brand new, they were new to me. Aunt Lottie made it an adventure as we shopped. We would take turns making up a story about the previous owners. It was so much fun.

My mother drove us to the Parkington shopping center in Ballston, Virginia.

She explained, "This was the area that she grew up around. Some of my uncles worked there when the shopping center first opened. Parkington was anchored by the headquarters location of the Hecht company and had the largest parking garage in the United States."

I showed little interest because I didn't want to be there. Every store we went to, my mother would pick out dresses and ask me to try them on. And every time I had to tell her that I did not like wearing dresses.

"I only wear jeans, tee shirts, sweaters, and sweatsuits."

"Raynelle, I really think your wardrobe should change since you are attending high school now."

We finally compromised and I let her pick out three pairs of slacks with matching blouses.

When my mother and I came back from shopping, I was putting away my new clothes and noticed a scrapbook on my bed. This scrapbook contained a copy of every award I had ever received for the past five years. It also had copies of all my report cards.

There were pictures from different events like my birthdays, holidays, and field trips. I thought about what my father had said in his letter, that my mother really had wanted to be a part of my life. Out of all the expensive presents she had given me, this scrapbook was priceless. I appreciated the scrapbook and vowed that I would keep it forever. Now I had a chance to add to it living once again with my mother.

After that day, I started showing her my gratitude by calling her momma. Whenever I had the opportunity, I would hug her and say "I love you." I had to admit to myself that it was impressive to have a mother that everyone else called Dr. Rowell.

My mother rearranged her client's appointments so she could drive me to school and pick me up most days. On the days that she couldn't drive me to school, I would ride public transportation. My mother said that when I turned sixteen years old she would buy me a car.

The second year after living with my mother, I mentioned to her that I didn't know anything about her life.

"Can you tell me about your childhood and how you met my father?" She started telling me her life story.

My mother Lauretta Ann (Rowell) Young was born in Ballston, Virginia, to Luke Anthony and Louise Mae (Stuart) Rowell. Grandpa Luke was ten years older than Grandma Louise. My mother was born the seventh of ten children.

The entire Rowell family had a distinct eye color. Their eye color changed with their moods. Light brown was the normal color, light gray, was the color when they were sick. Their eye color changed to hazel when they were angry.

This brought back the memory of one time my mother thought she had won an argument with my father but he told me later that it scared him whenever my mother's eye color changed. He would just walk away so he wouldn't see it. I have to admit that the first time I saw them change I was intimidated also. We laughed about this. It was good to laugh with her again.

My mother had very humble beginnings. They were poor but had more than most families. My mother was very sickly as a child because she suffered from a burning sensation in her feet and throbbing earaches. Grandma Louise put cotton balls in my mother's ears, especially if the wind was blowing. This helped her to sleep better. My mother found out later in life that she had neuropathy caused by a vitamin deficiency. Once she started taking vitamin B12, the pain was more tolerable.

The area they lived in was rural, so my grandmother had a vegetable garden and also raised chickens and pigs. My grandfather was a very stern man. He didn't allow any cooking on Sundays; all cooking had to be done on Saturdays. Grandma Louise was a good cook, but some said that Grandpa Luke's cooking was better. He usually was the one who did the cooking on Saturdays.

On Sundays, the whole family got up, prayed before breakfast, and went to church. I think we didn't go much because my mother was forced to go to church a lot as a child. As a family, we mostly went to church for funerals and weddings.

Grandpa Luke couldn't afford a car, so most of the transportation was done by walking or catching the Fairfax trolley that linked Fairfax, Vienna, and Ballston with downtown Washington, D.C. At this location, the railway built a car barn, rail yard, workshops, electrical substation, and a general office. Grandpa Luke and her older brothers, John, Stephen, and Thomas worked there. Her brothers moved out of the house once they were grown. Stephen went to war in Vietnam, but he made it back safe.

Grandpa Luke was a bricklayer and a good provider, even with so many children. He was a living example of loving-kindness with our neighbors. My mother said even though they didn't have much, Grandpa Luke made sure that no one went hungry in their neighborhood.

Grandma Louise at times could have a mean attitude. She was the oldest of several siblings. It wasn't uncommon in those days for someone to be illiterate as children left school to work or help out at home.

Even though the Rowell family lived in a nice framed house, there was no electricity. They used kerosene lamps. Their house only had two large rooms. Grandma Louise and the girls slept in one room; Grandpa Luke and the boys slept in the other room. Each sibling had a chore to do. The two oldest sisters, Hannah and Sarah, were to fill the kerosene lamps and cook for the family. Sarah was very lazy, which caused friction with Hannah. My mother and her brother, Matthew, brought in wood for the stove to heat the house.

My mother's sister, Esther, died at the early age of ten from pneumonia. Grandpa Luke couldn't afford to take her to the hospital. Everyone took it very hard, especially Grandma Louise. Esther's body was kept in their house for viewing until the funeral. She was buried at the family church cemetery.

My mother was teased a lot because she was skinny and had long legs. Her nickname was *Ichabod Crane* from the book *Sleepy Hollow*. She was a tomboy who could hit a baseball harder and climb higher than any boy. Grandpa Luke only raised his voice when he was angry, but Grandma Louise did most of the disciplining. My mother said that she only got two whippings. The first whipping she got was for fighting a boy. The other whipping was for making a girl take off a dress given to her by Grandma Louise.

My mother was eighteen when her father died. She wanted to go into the Army after his death. She asked her mother for her blessing. Although my mother was old enough that she didn't need her permission, her mother would not give her blessing. She said the military was no place for her. The guy my mother was dating at the time was moving back to New York, so she decided to go with him. I think she was trying to hurt her mother. My mother admitted she got homesick after a few months and came back to Virginia.

After several months of being unemployed, my mother decided to become a dental assistant after seeing an ad in the newspaper. She scored so high on the admission exam that she received a scholarship for the dental school. When my mother finished school, she decided to move with a cousin in Washington, D.C.

It was a new world for her. Not having to watch any siblings, not having to share a bed with someone, and not having to go to church every Sunday. My mother did like singing in the church choir, but the trip took too long to go back and forth for rehearsals.

She had so much freedom. My mother's cousin, Kimberly Hall, was pretty but not as beautiful as my mother. My mother was dark-skinned and had a glow about her. Every Saturday night, they would get dressed up and catch a bus to Georgetown. There were so many clubs that each weekend they picked a different club to check out.

One Saturday, my father was playing at the club they went to. My mother told her cousin that she had seen him before in the neighborhood.

"You are kidding," her cousin Kimberly said. "I never saw him before."

"That's because you don't go to the grocery store. You depend on me to buy all the food."

"Well, we all have to do our part. I might start going now."

The next time my mother went to the grocery store, she introduced herself.

"Hi, my name is Lauretta Rowell. I heard you playing at the club last Saturday. You are very talented."

"Thanks." My father said, not even looking up. He just kept bagging her groceries.

After he finished bagging he asked her, "Do you need help to your car?"

"No, I'm walking," she said.

Chapter 3 : Changed Heart

He smiled, "Okay, I'm going on break now."

The cashier told my mother, "You are wasting your time. All Joseph cares about is working. I think all he does is work."

As my mother walked home, she made a promise to herself that she was going to go out with him. She presumed this was going to be a challenge.

The following Saturday, my mother and Kimberly went back to the club to hear my father play. When he took his break at the bar, she tried to buy him a drink.

"I don't drink when I'm playing because it messes with my concentration," he said.

"I totally understand. Maybe I can buy you one after you finish playing."

"No." He said, "I'm going straight home."

My mother went back to the table where Kimberly sat. Kimberly was at the table with a guy, so my mother went back to the bar until she was ready to go home.

My father was truly a good trumpeter and singer. You could feel his passion as he played. Once he finished his set, my mother was ready to go. She went back to the table to get Kimberly. The guy that she was with didn't want her to go. Fiercely he reached out and grabbed her arm.

"Where do you think you are going? I bought you two drinks."

Kimberly asked him, "Do you think you now own me?"

My mother thought to herself, *this guy doesn't know Kimberly's temper*. She had seen her take on guys twice her size. Kimberly was the only girl with four brothers. She learned at an early age how to defend herself.

My mother spoke to him, "What's your name?"

"It's Larry," he angrily replied.

"Hey Larry, let me buy you a drink."

"No." He replied, "I want this tease to buy me one."

Kimberly got up and stood over him with both hands on her hips and said, "Who are you calling a tease?"

She took what was left of her drink and threw it right in Larry's face. Larry jumped up and his chair fell backward on the floor. He had his fist balled up.

My father came from out of nowhere and stood in between Larry and Kimberly.

"Hey man, chill out. We don't want any trouble here. See that bouncer over there? He hasn't thrown anyone out all night. You wouldn't want to be the first would you?"

"No, " Larry replied. "She's not even worth it."

Quickly, Larry left the club.

My mother told him, "I'm so sorry you got in the middle of that."

"I can't stand to see any man lose his cool. I hate it even worse when a man acts like he going to hit a woman. Where I came from, men did not hit women."

My mother thanked him again. "I had better get my cousin home before she makes a fool of herself again."

Kimberly had a slur in her words when she said, "I'm no fool. I was going to kick his butt!"

My Papa offered to get them a taxi. As they each took Kimberly's arms to walk her out of the club and to a taxi, my mother told him, "I'll see you soon at the grocery store."

"Okay; sure. Next time."

My mother thought to herself that he was talented, handsome, and a gentleman. Kimberly fell asleep as soon as they got in the taxi. As they arrived home, my mother stumbled out of the taxi with Kimberly and got them both into the apartment. She was so glad that there were not a lot of steps.

Two weeks later, my mother went to the grocery store. My father actually spoke to her first.

"How is your cousin? She hasn't thrown any more drinks lately has she?"

"No, not yet."

"I got another job at a different club. Maybe one night the two of you can stop by and give me some support."

"That sounds cool," my mother told him and he wrote down the address.

She said, "I'll keep a closer eye on Kimberly next time."

The cashier's mouth dropped open when my father gave her the club's address. My mother just winked at the cashier as she left the store.

The next time my mother got paid she bought a new dress, new shoes, and got her hair done. Kimberly gave her a manicure and pedicure.

"That's the least you can do after embarrassing me."

Kimberly teased my mother, "I hope you didn't waste your money on this makeover because Joseph doesn't look like he is interested in you."

"Well, Ms. Know-It-All," my mother replied, "if he wasn't interested, why did he invite us to a club tonight?"

They dated for six months before my mother took my father to Virginia to meet Grandma Louise. It seemed that Grandma Louise had gotten meaner since Grandpa Luke's death. She didn't like my father because he was fair-skinned and he had a New Orleans accent. My mother was very independent-minded except when it came to her mother. She was always looking for her approval.

Grandma Louise had a fit when my father said he seldom went to church. She wasn't showing any love towards him like the Bible said to do. She was being a real hypocrite. My father saw how uncomfortable her mother was making her, so he made an excuse for them to leave.

Chapter 3 : Changed Heart

Kimberly had gone out of town, so she asked my father in for a drink. They got really drunk and, in the end, I was conceived that night. When my mother told my father, that she was pregnant, he was excited. He felt that this was his second chance to have a family. My father asked her to marry him.

My mother told me she said yes because she didn't want to be like her youngest sister, Madeline, who had a baby out of wedlock. Grandma Louise had told the whole family not to acknowledge Madeline or the child ever. My mother didn't listen to her. She was the only relative that kept in touch with Madeline.

When my mother told Grandma Louise that she was getting married she asked her if she was pregnant. She said yes because she couldn't lie. Immediately, Grandma Louise told her that she didn't ever want to see that heathen, bastard child, or her ever again. My mother was heartbroken. My father tried to console her but to no avail.

They got married by the local Justice of the Peace. Uncle Claude, Aunt Lottie, and Kimberly were the only witnesses. My mother got another job closer to the grocery store.

She didn't realize my father was a frugal person until after they got married. He counted every penny. If she went over the budget, he would have a tantrum. My mother wasn't used to budgeting. She was a free spender who often spent more than she made.

After I was born, my father got worse. He was saving for a house, which was why he had taken on two jobs. My mother thought he would quit playing at the club after they got married, but he refused.

My mother grew to hate living over the grocery store. However, my father and I made the best of it. He would tell me to use my imagination and pretend every week that we lived somewhere different in the world. This didn't work for my mother. She accused my father of mindless babble and said that he was too cheap to take a vacation.

My mother stated she saw so much more potential in my father than he saw in himself. She tried to encourage him to play music professionally. However, he had lost his zeal and made excuses not to become anything else. She got so frustrated with him that her love became resentment and then turned to bitterness. She thought that she would finish her degree in dentistry, but she lost her scholarship. It was hard being married and being a mother. Finally, she was able to get a job as a dental hygienist.

My mother deeply cared about my father when they got married, but she just wasn't in love with him. She didn't believe in abortion, yet she didn't want to attempt to raise a child by herself. She was much too selfish for that. My mother had seen all that Madeline went through being a single mom. Because my mother had a great rapport with the dentist she worked for, she was able to bring me to work. The entire staff helped her with me. This went on until I turned five years old. Then I started school.

My parents were always arguing. My mother kept bringing home various expensive gifts. My mother always told my father that a patient had given it to her. But I had known better. I always thought my mother was a flirt before we went to New Orleans. She would always have a meeting once a week with the dentist behind closed doors. She would always come out fixing her hair and uniform. Most of the time she had a little gift bag in her hand.

Infidelity from my mother was bound to happen because their marriage relationship was cold and distant. Secrecy made her excited. What respect my father had toward my mother was slowly replaced with contempt.

Biblical Characters For Chapter Three

"For whatever was previously written was written for our instruction, so that through perseverance and encouragement of the Scriptures we might have Hope."
     -Romans 15:4

Grandma Louise And Miriam

Grandma Louise Rowell had Hope in herself as the matriarch because she was domineering to her family. The Bible gives the account of Miriam, who had similar life events as Grandma Louise (in Numbers 12).

Grandma Louise and Miriam were women who had a relationship with God. But they did not imitate God when it came to their relationships with their families. Both women caused division in their families by their interpretation of God's Word.

Grandma Louise's behavior caused her to be estranged from two of her daughters for years. Miriam was jealous of her brother, Moses, and encouraged their other brother, Aaron, to be against him also. Grandma Louise and Miriam eventually were reunited with their families.

The Story of Miriam

Miriam's role as a prophetess and worship leader suggests that, while some denominations may have trouble with women holding important leadership positions, God does not. The fact that Miriam was a prophetess illustrates that God speaks to the whole community of faith through women as well as through men.

Miriam's faults teach us as much as her gifts. As a religious leader, she knew better than to criticize Moses. Miriam dishonored God and Moses who had more of an intimate relationship than her. People in a position of leadership have an extra responsibility to honor God. God expects those He puts in leadership positions to humble themselves and to honor Him.

Miriam reminds us that jealousy and pride stand in the way of our fellowship with God. Those traits also prevent God from using us to minister to others.

We are to rejoice in the gifts God gives us and use them carefully. Comparing ourselves to others is dangerous and wrong. We can feel fulfillment in serving wherever we are. We need not feel belittled if we do not have gifts or positions that others enjoy.

Many times, wives or families of religious leaders will be unfairly criticized. It is better to focus on Christ's example of love and his acceptance of others than follow Miriam's negative example.

> "The eye of the Lord is on those who fear Him, on those who Hope in His loving-kindness."
> -Psalm 33:18

Grandpa Luke And Caleb

Grandpa Luke Rowell had Hope in God giving him instructions on how to be a good provider for his family. The Bible gives the accounts of Caleb who had similar life events as Grandpa Luke:

- Numbers 13:1–6, 26–33; 14:6–10, 24–38; and 32:11–12;
- Joshua 14:6–15 and 15:13-20;

- Judges 1:12– 15)

Grandpa Luke and Caleb were strong-willed men who planned for the future of their families. They didn't look at their present circumstances but what could be by having Hope and faith in God.

The Story of Caleb

Caleb served as one of the twelve tribal leaders commissioned as spies by Moses to survey the Promised Land after the exodus from Egypt. Ten of the twelve spies frightened the Israelites with reports from Canaan of fortified cities and gigantic people. Compared to the giants on land, they saw themselves as grasshoppers.

Caleb and Joshua also saw the fortified cities in the land, but they reacted in faith rather than fear. They advised Moses, Aaron, and the Israelites to attack Canaan immediately.

The Israelites listened to the negative report of the ten spies rather than Caleb and Joshua. The Lord viewed their fear as a lack of faith and judged them for their spiritual cowardice. All the adults alive at that time died in the wilderness for their lack of faith in God's promises. Only Caleb and Joshua would live to possess the land.

At eighty-five years of age and after forty years of wandering in the wilderness, faithful Caleb received his long-awaited divine inheritance. Hebron became his territory in the Promised Land.

Chapter 3 : Changed Heart

Chapter 4

The Academy Chronicles

I never knew what to expect the days when I rode the public bus to school. There were either ordinary days or days of utter chaos. By car, the Academy is approximately an hour drive from our house, while commuting by bus adds thirty minutes to the ride because of the many stops.

One morning, a woman was trying to run across the street to catch the bus and got hit by a car. It was not for the fainthearted to see her lay prone in the street. This incident caused me to be late for school.

Another time, there was a pregnant woman who went into labor on the bus. Luckily, a nurse going to work assisted her until the ambulance came. Again, I was late for school. As I walked to the administrative office, I anticipated a judgmental expression from the secretary who had to give me an admittance slip to class.

During one bus ride home from school, a man who had dementia got on the bus and became very agitated. He was causing much turmoil. Some of the men on the bus had to restrain him until the police came. After a few months on the bus, I became acquainted with the bus driver and some of the regular riders.

Mr. Brown became my favorite passenger. He rode the bus at least once a week. He was blind but he had a service dog named Max to assist him. Mr. Brown didn't want any help getting on and off the bus or finding a seat. One morning, Max led Mr. Brown to the only seat left, which was beside me. Max started rubbing his head against my hand and Mr. Brown could feel what Max was doing, so he reprimanded him.

"Max, it's rude to intrude on another person's space."

"That's alright. I always wanted a dog," I told Mr. Brown. My parents had agreed on no pets because they both were too busy and I was too young to care for a dog.

The next time I saw Mr. Brown and Max, I had some doggie treats with me. I asked Mr. Brown if I could give some to Max and he agreed. I finally introduced myself to the two after that day. Max intentionally would look for me when they got on the bus.

"Max is attracted to the smell of strawberries," Mr. Brown said.

"I like chewing strawberry gum. Sometimes I forget to spit it out before class and then I get detention."

"My mother used to cook strawberry pies." He explained to me that his other senses (smell, hearing, taste, and touch) were enhanced due to his blindness.

I adored Mr. Brown because he would reminiscence about his childhood antics. Mr. Brown shared that when he was about seven years old, his brother who was three years older than him came up with a scheme to get money. He would intentionally have Mr. Brown get hit by a door or grocery cart so he could fall down. Mr. Brown would then pretend that he hit his head on the ground and couldn't see. His brother would then cause a big commotion. The person who hit him or a store manager would offer his brother money to go away with no concern for Mr. Brown's well-being.

Then, when he got older, his brother decided to use cars. He would time it so just before a car stop at a red light Mr. Brown would fall in front of the car. His brother would then scream, "My brother was hit by the car and now he is blind!" When his brother would threaten to call the police, the drivers would offer money for them to leave the scene—again with no concern for his well-being.

They did this scam for a couple of months until the pastor from their neighborhood was involved. The pastor knew Mr. Brown was already blind. He told them to get in his car. He drove them home and told their mother what they had been doing.

"My mother gave us the worst whipping that we had ever had. I can still feel the belt on my rear end," Mr. Brown said.

"That's why I'm so bitter toward people. Those scams showed how people don't have kindness for one another and how cons can take advantage of this."

One day, I asked Mr. Brown, "Where are you going?"

He said, "We ride the bus to the end of the line and then transfer to another bus that takes us to Maryland." Mr. Brown confessed that he visits his brother at a correctional institute.

"My brother stayed in trouble and, when he turned sixteen, he dropped out of school and joined a gang. During a robbery, he was the driver for the gang when he hit and killed a little girl." Mr. Brown's brother was sentenced to life in prison. He had forgiven his brother for all of the times he used him.

"My brother had no one else in the world that cared about him."

Chapter 4 : The Academy Chronicles

I felt so out of my comfort zone at the Academy. I missed my former school, Mrs. Davis, and her daughters, Karen and Sharon. I often felt desolate because I didn't make friends easily. I wished that I was more like my parents. Both of them could blend into almost any environment.

I was also intimidated because the majority of the students at the Academy were from wealthy families. Their parents were either lawyers, doctors, ambassadors, entertainers, or athletes. Some of my classmates arrived and departed by chauffeured cars— Bentley, Rolls Royce, and Mercedes Benz.

When the time came for me to fill out my class schedule, I tried to pick the hardest classes. Almost every day, I was the first to finish my school work. I never tried to disturbed anyone. I would take out a book to read. I enjoyed reading because then I could visualize myself all over the world. I could experience different things and places in the book that I may never get to see in person.

My American Literature teacher, Mrs. Potts, would seek to make an example of me. She would say, "Raynelle finished her homework on time" or "Raynelle got another A." This led to isolation from my peers.

A group of three girls started bullying me. The leader of this entourage was Amber Greene. She was the spoiled daughter of Mr. Greene, a former Broadway actor. Her parents were divorced so her father usually gave her whatever she wanted. Amber stayed with her father during the school year and then went to New York with her mother during the summer.

Amber and her two friends had known each other for years. They ate lunch together and had most of the same classes. Amber would start by murmuring sarcastic remarks about my clothes. I mostly liked to wear jeans and sweat pants. Amber would continually ask me, "Do you have a deep desire to be a boy?" She said that because she overheard my mother call me Ray instead of Raynelle. I just ignored her, but then I started finding notes inside my locker. *Your kind isn't welcomed in the Academy.* During gym class, they would tell me to use the boy's locker room because they didn't want me staring at them. I forged a letter from my mother to excuse me from the gym because of the bullying.

Daily I spent my lunchtime in the library. The librarian would tease me saying, "At the rate of your reading, I am going to run out of books." Reading was a way to escape from the issues of my life. My excitement for learning and loving books came from my mother. When I was younger, we spent time together and she would read to me for hours. My mother would tell me that if you can use your imagination you can be anywhere in the world.

One morning, Mr. Brown sensed something was wrong because I wasn't talkative. I didn't even play with Max. I told him, "I just have a lot on my mind." He kept pressing the issue until I told him about Amber. Mr. Brown insisted that when I got home from school I should tell my mother everything. He said I was too young to carry this burden alone. I reluctantly agreed to tell my mother about the bullying.

When I got home, my mother was with a patient. As I waited for her, Aunt Lottie called. She could tell from my voice that something was wrong.

"I miss you so much, Aunt Lottie. Sometimes I feel so alone."

"Are you going to church?"

"We haven't been to church since Papa's funeral." She told me to still read my Bible that she gave me and that I could watch sermons on the TV until we find a church. I promised her that I would try. I then told Aunt Lottie what I was going through at school.

"There will be ruthless people who cause disrupting confrontations throughout your whole life. You are a special young lady. Let your focus decide your feelings. If you focus on how someone else feels about you then you will always feel less than them. People only have control over you if you let them and there should be only two viewpoints about yourself that matter— God's and yours. God's viewpoint is that you were fearfully and wonderfully made for a purpose. Finding your purpose is the journey and true joy of life."

Aunt Lottie said, "I'm proud of you because you didn't stay in the familiar but ventured out into the unfamiliar. Ray, you have just as much right to be at that school as anyone else. Stay the course and see where this journey will go."

"Ray, I pray for you every day. Remember that God loves you." After speaking with her, I always felt comforted. I was determined to look at things differently. Aunt Lottie also demanded that I tell my mother about the bullying.

I decided to speak to Mrs. Potts first instead of my mother. She didn't realize that the recognition of my grades and homework actually caused a problem. Mrs. Potts submitted a written notice to the freshman counselor about our conversation. I had no idea that Mrs. Potts had submitted this until my mother received an official letter stating that I had a counseling appointment. My mother was very disappointed that I hadn't come to her about the bullying.

I told her, "I was trying to avert your involvement because you were busy."

"I thought by now, Ray, that you know you come first." I apologized and explained everything that had been going on with Amber. I didn't want her to feel more disappointed, so I didn't mention that I spoke with Aunt Lottie.

The counseling appointment usually consisted of a small group. Included in this appointment were the counselor, Mr. Bridges, Amber, and her two friends with their parents, my mother, and me. Mr. Greene is on the executive board for the Academy. Mr. Bridges explained to the parents why they were there. The girls denied all of it.

Mr. Bridges said, "I have statements from other students that these facts are true." Amber wanted their names.

Mr. Bridges said, "According to the school's policy, that is confidential information." Mr. Bridges had taken great lengths to change all of our class schedules so we would not be in the same classes or lunch together.

My mother suggested the students wear school uniforms. Mr. Bridges stated, "It would be too expensive to change the school's policy." Mr. Greene agreed with my mother, but he was busy watching her legs. I could see where the entourage got their traits from because their parents agreed with Mr. Greene. Mr. Greene said he would make that recommendation to the Academy's executive board at their next meeting. Amber protested but her father didn't care.

It was during my junior year at the Academy that the dress code was changed. It was a long process to choose the color and what uniform company to award the contract to. Mr. Greene recommended my mother to be on the committee to make these decisions. He tried relentlessly to get a date with her. I'm so glad she turned him down. My mother said, "There are three reasons I won't go out with him. First, he is too arrogant. Second, Amber is his daughter and, third, I don't find him attractive."

My mother did get her recommendation of Fridays being a dress-down day. Students were allowed to wear other clothes instead of uniforms. I was ecstatic that I could go back to my jeans and sweat pants. I didn't have to worry that Amber would blame me for the dress code change because her father took the credit claiming that it was his idea.

During my freshman class registration, I had seen a class entitled *Imagine That*. It was a drama class that also included learning how to be a stage manager. Mr. Jackson taught the class. He had attended the Academy as a student. He went to New York for college and came back to the school to teach. This was his first teaching job.

Mr. Jackson encouraged his students to think outside the box. He would tell us to be inventive. He reminded me of a younger version of my father. I asked him, "Are you from New Orleans?" He was a native of Washington, D.C. like me.

Clearly, he was the most popular teacher. I think it had a lot to do with how he talked with his students. Not only was he good-looking, but he talked with us and never down to us. I personally felt that I could talk to him about anything. Before meeting Mr. Jackson, I didn't trust any other male except Uncle Claude.

It took me a while to notice a boy who got off the bus at the Academy the same time I did. I could see that he was shyer than I. I found out his name was Derek Frazer. Derek and his mother lived in the southeast section of Washington, D.C. He rode the subway from his house and then caught the bus to the Academy. His father had been in the U.S. Army but was killed in Afghanistan. Through a military support group, Derek received a scholarship to the Academy. Since the rape incident with my evil brothers, Derek was the first boy my age that I felt comfortable with.

Derek became my best and only friend at the Academy. It seemed we had a lot in common. We loved to read mystery novels, play chess, watch old black-and-white movies, listen to Motown music, and cook. Derek was overweight, wore braces, and looked like a geek. He reminded me of the cartoon character, Fat Albert, and Urkel on the Family Matters television series. His hobbies were programming computers and watching cooking shows.

Derek and I started hanging out on weekends because his mother worked two jobs. We took turns cooking for each other. My mother always looked forward to Derek's turn to cook. Derek introduced my mother to tofu. He would create a different tofu dish for her. Derek loved doing special things for others.

The second year at the Academy, I convinced Derek to also enroll in the Imagine That class. He was reluctant at first. However, Derek's mentor, Mr. Cooper, was in the army and he encouraged him to do it also. When Mr. Jackson found out how good Derek was with machines, he appointed Derek to be the technical director. This meant Derek would operate the controls for the lights and sounds. This was the first chance for Derek to overcome his shyness. I could see that being around Mr. Cooper, Derek had gained more confidence in himself. He also began working on his appearance.

When I turned sixteen, my mother offered to buy me a car. I refused her offer and explained that I wanted to be independent and buy my own first car. I was planning to use some of my father's life insurance money. My mother was disappointed that I didn't want a new car. My mother said she wanted me to be realistic and think long-term. I reassured her that I had done some research and knew which cars were reliable. My mother finally agreed as long as we went to her client who owned a used car lot.

So, we went there and I bought myself a used purple Volvo sedan. I named the car Barney. Barney had black leather seats, a built-in cassette deck, and an AM/FM radio. I was just happy to have transportation to get me from point A to point B. The first time Derek saw it he said, "That looks like a purple dinosaur." Once the new school year started, Derek would catch the bus as usual to the subway station. Then I would pick him up from the station and drive him to school. I felt so independent.

For three years, in Mr. Jackson's class, I only got small parts in plays. However, I never wanted a lead part. I was happy to have any part. I didn't play an instrument, but I could sing. I even developed the confidence to sing in public.

Every year, Mr. Jackson would have a contest in each of his six classes to create the best-written play. Then, from the six winners, all of the classes would vote on which play would be used as a fundraiser for the school. Mr. Jackson assigned us into teams of four. Derek and I were part of a team together. The play carried half of our grade. The winners could be the lead characters or we could pick someone else to act those parts.

Our team won the contest for the class we were in. We had collaborated to write a jazz musical of the play *Romeo and Juliet*. Instantaneously, I was noticed for something positive since attending the Academy. Different peers would wish our team good luck in the vote. I was excited. To my surprise, out of the six selections, we won the vote! This meant our musical would be performed as the spring fundraiser. I called my mother and she said that we would celebrate when I got home from school.

It was now senior year at the Academy and my foe, Amber Greene, was the most popular student. She was the head cheerleader, class president, and now she wanted the lead part in our musical. Our paths hadn't crossed since freshman year. Her father, Mr. Greene, always volunteered to be the director of the fundraiser play. The lead character had to be a soprano. Amber tried her best to get me to pick her as my lead character because her boyfriend, Duke Morgan, had been chosen to be Romeo. Duke was on academic probation from the football team. Performing in the play allowed him to earn extra credit so that he could get reinstated to the football team. A student was allowed to practice a sport but not play in games. Any student on academic probation also could not participate in extracurricular activities, such as class trips and dances.

Just about every girl at the Academy had a crush on Duke. Amber had always had Duke and now three girls in her entourage. They followed her everywhere she went. She tried flattery, presents, and bribery to convince me to choose her for the lead. I didn't want Duke in the play, but since Derek was the technical director, he couldn't be in the play also. Mr. Jackson chose Duke. So Amber got the lead part and I became her understudy.

Mr. Jackson also selected me to be the stage manager for the musical. One day, while working on a prop for the play, Amber was goofing around with her friends backstage, which was against the rules. Amber always just ignored any rule and did what she wanted to do. I tried to get her attention, but she was too intense with her conversation. Amber backed up, tripped over me, and fractured her ankle. Mr. Jackson came to render help and had someone run to the office for the nurse and call an ambulance.

When Amber finally came back to school, she accused me of causing her accident on purpose so I could get the lead to the play. She said, "You have a crush on Duke and wanted a chance to get close to him."

Making that false accusation was not enough for Amber. She started rumors that Mr. Jackson and I were sexually intimate. My peers started whispering about me. They said, "Raynelle only got into the Academy because her mother slept with the principal." I also found notes in my locker stating that my mother and I were tramps. The bullying got worse. I started receiving vulgar notes inside my school locker. Then a fake picture of Mr. Jackson and me in a compromising position was posted on the school bulletin board.

The principal saw the school bulletin board and called my mother in for a meeting. My mother was aware of everything before the principal called because Mr. Jackson had warned her. My mother brought her lawyer, Mr. David Williams with her to the meeting.

Mr. Williams told the principal it was in his best interest that he find out who was behind everything. He reminded him of the positive reputation of the Academy and commented that this would be a great human interest story to the press.

Amber had so much control over her entourage that she convinced one of the girls to confess. Finally, Amber had her other two friends lie about Mr. Jackson to get him fired. They accused him of making sexual advancements toward them. Mr. Greene told Mr. Jackson in confidence that he believed Amber was behind everything, but he couldn't prove it yet. Amber had her friends so intimidated they wouldn't dare turn against her. Mr. Greene convinced the executive board to let Mr. Jackson be suspended with pay while the investigation went on. The board also decided to cancel the musical for the fundraiser.

I was so glad that spring break was the following week. When classes resumed, I could concentrate on my grades. Until then, I felt like my life was ripped apart again. I thought I would be able to be strong like Aunt Lottie told me, but I couldn't. I started throwing up and having anxiety attacks.

The final straw was when someone covered Barney with eggs, spray-painted the word tramp on the back, and let the air out of my tires. I called my mother, crying. She told me to use my camera to take pictures at every angle. Derek and some other students were there too. My mother had the car towed and she came and picked me up. Mr. Williams threatened to sue the school and the board. I asked Mr. Williams if he could arrange for me to be schooled at home for the last semester.

Mr. Jackson felt that everything was his fault. However, my mother assured him that nothing was his fault. Mr. Jackson volunteered to teach me the rest of the semester and administer all of my final tests. The Academy agreed to everything because they were already getting bad press. Mr. Jackson and I learned more about each other while he was teaching me. I shared with him about the incident with my brothers and how my father became overprotective. Mr. Jackson told me that he admired that I was able to get through all that hurt. He thought I had an inner strength that most people didn't have. I told him it was only because of Aunt Lottie's strong faith in God.

Mr. Jackson explained that he was from a long line of preachers. He said his father wanted him to become the fourth-generation preacher of the family. It wasn't until this year that his father finally accepted the fact that he didn't want to be a preacher. Mr. Jackson had convinced his father that his chosen occupation, teaching, gave him the chance to be a positive influence over young people's destiny.

Derek had started eating his lunch under the bleachers in the gym. One day, Amber and Duke came in and sat right above him. They were unaware that he was there. They were talking about Mr. Jackson and me. Derek started recording the conversation on his cassette recorder that he sometimes took to class.

Duke was pleading with Amber to tell the truth about everything. Amber was ignoring him. Duke threatened Amber by telling her that if she didn't tell the truth, he was going to break up with her. Amber spoke up then and said that she was only going out with him because he was the most popular boy in school. She also told him that she could always find another dumb jock. Amber loudly hobbled out of the gym on her crutches. Derek dropped his phone and Duke heard it.

Duke looked under the bleachers and saw him. Duke told him, "You can come out." Duke started telling Derek, "I feel so guilty about what Amber did to Mr. Jackson and Raynelle. I knew what was going on but did not say anything." Duke confessed to him, "You see, Ray was secretly tutoring me."

I had made sure Duke only came over on the Saturdays that Derek didn't come. Duke had lied to Amber on those Saturdays telling her that he had to take his grandmother shopping and anywhere else she needed to go.

Duke said, "Ray has been more of a friend to me than I have been to her. If it wasn't for her, I would not be back on the football team. You know what? Use that recording to bust Amber and her entourage. Do what you have to do."

After school, Derek came over to my house and made cassette copies of the conversation. He made one copy for my mother and another for Mr. Williams. Mr. Williams called the principal immediately for a meeting.

One of the members of the Academy executive board was a retired police sergeant. He interviewed each one of Amber's friends along with their parents. They cracked and snitched that Amber came up with the idea to lie against Mr. Jackson and me. One of them did the fake photo picture that was posted on the bulletin board.

After the truth came out about Amber, her father forced her and the other girls to write formal apologies to Mr. Jackson and me. They were expelled from the Academy and had to attend summer classes in order to graduate from school elsewhere. All of Amber's ambitions were squashed. Mr. Greene made Amber pay for the repairs to Barney. The Academy offered Mr. Jackson reinstatement to his teaching job. He declined and started re-evaluating his personal life choices.

He decided to follow his passion for drama and opened a community theatre. My mother surprised me when she insisted that she be an investor for his theatre. Mr. Jackson said that his first production would be the play that we wrote in school. He also offered Derek and me jobs during our summer breaks from college. Derek and I were accepted to the same college in Pennsylvania.

During the whole incident at the Academy, my mother was making travel plans for us. She felt I deserved a memorable summer before leaving for college. She arranged for us to see places that I had only read about. It would also give us some time alone.

"This is a triple celebration. We are celebrating your high school graduation, eighteenth birthday, and college acceptance."

We had a small celebration at home with Ms. Bowman, Mr. Jackson, Mr. Williams, Derek, and his mom. It was great. Uncle Claude and Aunt Lottie sent me an expensive camera so that I could document our travels. Ms. Bowman gave me a pair of earrings with my birthstone. Derek gave me a journal to write about all of my adventures in. Mr. Williams gave me a $500 check. However, the most cherished gift of all came from Mr. Jackson.

My mother had given him two pictures of my father. Mr. Jackson had a gold heart locket made for me. On one side of the locket was my father playing his trumpet. On the other side was the last picture I took with my father. I couldn't hold back the tears.

After everyone left, I went to my room and looked at the scrapbook my mother had given me. When my mother came and checked on me, she brought our trip itinerary for me to look at. We were booked on the *Quest of Your Dreams* cruise. The itinerary included Barbados, South America, South Africa, South Asia, and many more places. I couldn't help but be excited about all of the places that we were going to.

My mother worked extra hard to make sure that all of her patients had their teeth cleanings completed. She had also arranged for a colleague to accept any dental emergencies. She was giving Ms. Bowman and her dental staff paid time off while we were gone.

Our cruise was booked for the second week in June and returned two weeks before classes would start at college. I did most of my packing for college before we left for Fort Lauderdale, Florida. Derek would be using my car, Barney, while my mother and I were traveling. The plan was to rent a trailer to transport all that we both were taken to Pennsylvania. I gave him a long list of what not to do while driving Barney.

"The way Barney is now is the way I expect to see him when I get back." I even made him sign a contract. My mother said, "You are being a little too obsessive." I felt that after the repairs to Barney, he was better than before.

Derek drove us to the airport to catch our flight to Fort Lauderdale, Florida. We stayed at a hotel for two days before our cruise was to depart. We went shopping the first day. My mother decided before we went on the trip to give me a full makeover. She said, "It is time to get away from your tomboy look of jeans and sweat pants." On the second day in Fort Lauderdale, we pampered ourselves to a manicure, pedicure, and massage.

My mother and I now had a lot of personal conversations. We got to know each other better.

"Do you ever think you will remarry?"

My mother took a deep sigh before she answered me. "Ray, I don't feel I deserve to be married again. I didn't appreciate or honor the relationship that I had with your father."

"Momma, you have proven that you have changed. You deserve happiness. I want you to start dating and I know who the first man should be."

"Who?" She asked, with a quaint look on her face.

"I see how Mr. Williams looks at you," I laughed.

"We actually have been out to a few business dinners."

"Well, it's time to step it up."

"Why look at this! My eighteen-year-old daughter is trying to give her mother advice about romance."

"Well," I said, "somebody's got to do it!" Then we both laughed.

"What about you?" She asked.

"What about me?"

"Ray, you have not dated anyone. You are a very beautiful and intelligent young lady."

"Momma," I sighed, "to be honest with you, I never thought seriously about getting close to any boy."

"What about Derek?"

"That's different. Derek is my best friend."

"Yes, and he is also a young handsome man."

"Momma, I love Derek like a brother!" I exclaimed.

"Well, Ray I am going to give you the same advice that you gave me," she smiled. "You should start dating once you get to college. Join some clubs and meet young men your age."

"I'll think about it."

During the cruise, I sent postcards from every exotic place we stopped at to Uncle Claude, Aunt Lottie, Derek, and Mr. Jackson. The *Quest of Your Dreams* ocean liner was powered by four diesel engines with two additional gas turbines used when extra power is required. The liner was wonderfully grand. It had the largest dance floor at sea, a luxury cinema, ten restaurants and bars, three swimming pools, two casinos, and the first-ever at-sea planetarium. There were many shopping boutiques centered around the ship's magnificent grand lobby.

The liner first sailed south to Barbados, which had the third oldest parliament in the world. Its capital is Bridgetown. One of the most inspiring experiences you can have in Barbados is participating in a sea turtle hatching release.

The ship then sailed by Devil's Island in French Guiana, South America, which was a famous prison of the 19th and 20th centuries. It was closed now. Then we passed Recife, which is the sixth-largest metropolitan area in Brazil. It is a major port on the Atlantic Ocean.

The ship docked in Rio De Janeiro for eight hours before continuing on the voyage. My mother and I had purchased tickets for a tour of the breathtaking views of Rio De Janeiro. I used my camera as we drove along. We saw the Corcovado Mountains and the famous landmark giant statue of Christ the Redeemer, which is recognized as one of the new Seven Wonders of the World. The tour guide pointed out the Sambadrome, which is a permanent grandstand-lined parade avenue for the annual colorful Carnival Parade. After four hours of riding, we stopped for lunch.

I had told my mother that I wanted to try each country's cuisine wherever we stopped. She was content because there was a Bistro that also had vegetable dishes. I ordered several appetizers so that I could taste a variety of dishes: bolinha de carne (fried meatballs), casquinho de caranguejo (crabmeat covered with brown manioc meal), pastel de camarao (a fried turnover stuffed with shrimps), and a salad. My mother ordered a fruit and vegetable platter. I told her, "You really don't know what you're missing." She replied, "I would rather live not to find out."

Our ocean liner embarked east to the remote island of St. Helena, so we were at sea for approximately three days. St. Helena is known as the island where Napoleon was exiled. It is a volcanic tropical island in the South Atlantic Ocean. We then traveled to Walvis Bay in Namibia, Africa. The Walvis Bay is rich in plankton and marine life, whose waters also drew in large numbers of southern right whales, attracting both whalers and fishing vessels.

We sailed for a couple of days before disembarking in Cape Town, which is a coastal city in South Africa. This city has several well-known natural features that attract tourists. Most notable is Table Mountain, which forms a large part of the Table Mountain National Park. Again, my mother and I took a bus tour. The tour guide spoke about Port Elizabeth, Durban, and Mozambique in South Africa, but going there would have taken more time than we had. Port Elizabeth was nicknamed the Friendly City or the Windy City. Durban, South Africa is the second-most important manufacturing hub in South Africa after Johannesburg. It is famous for being the busiest port in South Africa. Mozambique is endowed with many rich and extensive natural resources.

We went to a restaurant in Cape Town that had live music and storytelling while we ate. After the meal, we were entertained by marimba playing and interactive dancing. We met people from other countries, and the hostess was lovely. I ordered sosaties (South African lamb kebabs), oxtail potje with vegetables and, for dessert, a caramel fridge cake.

The *Quest of Your Dreams* continued to Maldives, which is a South Asian island country made up of many islands located in the Indian Ocean. This is where we disembarked again. In Maldives, fishing has historically been the dominant economic activity, followed by the rapidly growing tourism industry. In Maldives, we found a little diner to eat at. I ordered gulha (flour, tuna, and grated coconut), kavaaba (fish fritters), and rice. My mother ordered kattala (sweet potatoes), bambukeyo (breadfruit), and kashikeyo (screwpine).

When our ship arrived at Sri Lanka, my mother told me, "I had one dental mission trip here and several mission trips in the Southeast Asian countries of Malaysia, Singapore, and Vietnam." My mother was emotional when she told me, "Serving at these small remote villages made me appreciate what I had in the United States. It should be a requirement for all high school students to serve on a mission trip."

Sri Lanka has maritime borders with India to the northwest and the Maldives to the southwest. As a diverse and multicultural country, Sri Lanka is home to many religions, ethnic groups, and languages.

In Malaysia, we were able to see a traditional Malay musical performance. Singapore is the world's only island city that is populated with tropical flora, parks, and gardens. Singaporeans are mostly bilingual in the language of their mother tongue and with English as their common language.

The *Quest of Your Dreams* passed Vietnam before heading off to Shanghai. Shanghai is the second most populous city in China. In Shanghai, there are several museums of regional and national importance—the Shanghai Museum and the China Art Museum.

We took a U-turn this time and stopped at the ports of Hong Kong. Hong Kong is renowned for its deep natural harbor, which enables ready access by international cargo ships. My mother bought tickets for a day excursion to Ocean Park Hong Kong, which is a marine mammal park, aquarium, animal theme park, and amusement park.

During our cruise, there was a murder mystery night based on *Shadow of a Doubt*, an Alfred Hitchcock movie. I told my mother, "Derek is going to be so jealous when I tell him about this." The three-hour event was designed for uproarious laughter as we—the guests—tried to figure out who-done-it that night. The cruise cast selected members of the audience to play along and everyone was tasked with the challenge of solving the mystery and murder.

Anyone could be a part of the show, or you could put one of your friends or relatives into the mystery. The evening of who-done-it intrigue is set in a theater atmosphere full of comedy and audience interaction. The cast always kept you guessing as they helped advance the plotline and a detective lead the investigation to help you tie clues together and solve the mystery during the event.

The successful interactive mystery formula relied on information submitted from attending guests who either chose to be involved or wanted to set up one of their unsuspecting family members. Setting them up is a secret—and half of the fun. The cast even awarded prizes for some of the most correct and inventive answers to help solve the mystery.

After a few days at sea, the ocean liner then passed through the Suez Canal on its way to Corfu, before finally completing the journey in Venice. The months seemed to go by too fast. My mother and I had bonded more during the trip. We flew from Venice to New York and took a connecting flight to Maryland. After my mother and I picked up our luggage from the baggage claim and walked out of the airport, we saw Barney but did not see Derek.

Suddenly, this very handsome young man walked up and gave me a big hug. My mother and I both looked at each other. To our surprise, it was Derek! What a miraculous transformation he had made. His braces were off. Derek had lost at least 100 pounds. He was wearing contacts instead of glasses. We were speechless.

I felt something deep in the pit of my stomach. For the first time, I realized that I was attracted to Derek.

Chapter 4 : The Academy Chronicles

Biblical Characters For Chapter Four

"The Hope of the righteous will be gladness, but the expectation of the wicked will perish."
-Proverbs 10:28

Amber, Athaliah, And Potiphar's Wife

Amber Greene had Hope in herself because she manipulated everyone around her. The Bible gives the account of two women who had similar life events as Amber; Athaliah (in 2 Kings 8:26; 11:1–20; 2 Chronicles 22:10–12; 23:3–15, 21) and Potiphar's wife (in Genesis 39:1–20).

Amber, Athaliah, and Potiphar's wife were women who had disregard for other people to fulfill their selfish desires. These choices had a domino effect on the lives of people around them.

The Story of Athaliah

Athaliah was the daughter of King Ahab of Israel and Jezebel. Athaliah married Jehoram (or Joram), son of Jehoshapat, who was the King of Judah. Jehoram reigned only eight years and was succeeded by his son, Ahaziah, who died after reigning only one year. Athaliah apparently inherited Jezebel's ruthlessness. She was a tyrant whose every desire had to be obeyed. As her mother had done in Israel, Athaliah introduced Baal worship in Judah and, in so doing, destroyed part of the temple.

Desiring the throne for herself, Athaliah ruthlessly killed all of her grandsons. She succeeded with all but one-year-old Joash, who was taken into protective custody. In the seventh year, the high priest Jehoiada declared Joash the lawful king of Judah. Guards removed Athaliah from the temple before killing her to avoid defiling the temple with her blood. When Athaliah challenged this as treason, she was executed.

This woman serves as a warning that, when under stress, we may be tempted to do something we would never consider under normal circumstances. However, it is never right to do wrong. Ambition can be a positive thing, but Athaliah is an example of selfish ambition run riot. Whenever we consider doing wrong to achieve a personal goal, we need to remember this wicked queen's fate.

While Athaliah reminds us of the powerful influence parents have on their children, she reminds us that every person makes his or her own choices in life. While parents do influence their children, what parents cannot, and will not, determine is who their children will become. Athaliah gained the throne through murder and lost her life in the same way.

The Story of Potiphar's Wife

Joseph was the eleventh son of Jacob who had been sold into slavery by his brothers. He was taken to Egypt and purchased by an Egyptian named Potiphar. After Joseph displayed his abilities for managing Potiphar's household, he was promoted to oversee the entire estate.

Potiphar's wife played a small but notorious role in Joseph's life. Potiphar's wife became attracted to Joseph and attempted to seduce him. When Joseph refused her advances, she accused him of trying to rape her and Joseph was imprisoned.

All those who mistreat us, even the evil people we come in contact with, have a role in God's plan. This is important to remember when we encounter people like Potiphar's wife who caused one to suffer unjustly. We can still trust God, knowing that He is with us. We can still expect God to use our every experience to shape us for something in our future. We also can pity our persecutors, who mean to do us evil but are unaware that God is shaping us through every experience intending to do us good.

> "But the needy He saves from the sword, from their mouth, and from the hand of the mighty. So the helpless has Hope, and injustice shuts her mouth."
> -Job 5:15–16

Duke And Gideon

Duke Morgan's Hope was in correcting the wrong that Amber had done. The Bible gives the account of Gideon, who had similar life events as Duke (in Judges 6:11–8:29). Duke and Gideon were men who were the least to achieve anything great. When Duke made the choice to help Derek takedown Amber, it changed the lives of those she mistreated. Gideon's choice to obey and have Hope in God changed an entire nation.

The Story of Gideon

Gideon was a meek farmer who became a military hero and spiritual leader because he had delivered Israel from the oppression of the Midianites. As young Gideon was threshing wheat, the angel of the Lord appeared with strong words of encouragement. This angel announced that God had chosen

Gideon to deliver his people from the Midianites. Gideon then asked the messenger for a sign that God had selected him for a divine service. He prepared an offering and placed it on an altar. The angel touched the offering with his staff and fire consumed it. Gideon then recognized his personal call to serve God.

Gideon's first assignment was to destroy his father's altar to the pagan god Baal in the family's backyard. This act required great courage for Gideon feared his father's house and the men of the city who must have worshiped at that altar. For this reason, Gideon and ten of his servants destroyed the altar to Baal and cut down the Asherah pole beside it by night and erected an altar to the Lord. Gideon immediately presented an offering to the Lord on that altar.

When Gideon's fellow citizens discovered that the altar to Baal had been destroyed, they were outraged. When it was learned that Gideon the son of Joash has done this, Joash was called to account for his son's behavior. To his credit, Joash defended Gideon by implying that an authentic god should require no defense. If Baal is a god, let him plead for himself. So from that day, Gideon was called Jerubbaal, meaning to let Baal plead.

After that incident, Gideon raised an army to combat the Midianites. As the oppression of the Midianites intensified, Gideon sent out messengers to all of Manasseh and the surrounding tribes to rally volunteers to Israel's cause.

Gideon's volunteers assembled about 32,000 citizen soldiers. There were 135,000 Midianites camped in a nearby valley. God directed Gideon to thin out his men. After dismissing the fearful and afraid, only 10,000 soldiers remained. Gideon's army was now outnumbered about 13 to 1. God told Gideon that his army was still too large and He gave further instructions on how to decrease the army.

Gideon was to bring them down to the water, those who scooped up the water with their hands and never taking their eyes from the horizon were included in Gideon's army. Those who got down on their knees to drink and forgot to keep watch for the enemy were dismissed. Now only 300 soldiers remained. The Midianites outnumbered Gideon's band 450 to 1, but God and Gideon had a secret plan.

Gideon divided the army into three companies. Then he gave each man a trumpet, a pitcher, and a torch. At the appointed time, 300 trumpets blasted the air, 300 hands raised their pitchers and smashed them to bits, 300 burning torches pierced the darkness, and 300 warriors cried, "The sword of the Lord and of Gideon!"

The Midianites were thrown into panic. In the confusion, some committed suicide or killed their comrades. The remaining soldiers fled. The enemies of Israel were completely conquered and Israel's homeland was secured. It was a glorious victory for God and for Gideon, who became an instant hero. Gideon and his men pursued the fleeing enemy. Many of them were killed or captured by Gideon's allies.

As a conquering warrior, modest and devout, he was careful not to grasp at the power and glory that belonged to God. After the victory, Gideon was offered kingship but declined, taking instead payment in gold. He had been commissioned to lead his people away from idolatry and back to God.

After he retired to his home, Israel was blessed with forty years of peace. Through the life and exploits of Gideon, God had revealed much about Himself and the preparation that His leaders need for divine service. Gideon shows that God calls leaders from unlikely situations.

The story of Gideon also reminds us that God prefers, and needs, only a few dedicated and disciplined followers. His story is traditionally viewed as one of the prime examples of relying on the power of God even when circumstances and common sense might dictate another course of action.

Chapter 5

Secrets Exposed

Derek and I were both accepted to Mountain View College in Pennsylvania. He had enrolled in the computer science program and I was enrolled in creative arts. We had shared the cost of gas and the trailer to haul our things to Pennsylvania.

During the drive, I gave a narration of my summer travels. Derek divulged how he had lost the weight. He had created his own weight loss program on his computer. The program factored in calories burnt by exercise and his desired weight goal. He had also changed his eating habits.

Our dorms were on opposite sides of the campus. We unloaded his things first, then he came back with me to my dorm to unload my things. He was glad that he had brought a bike to get around the campus. When we got to my dorm room, I had a real surprise.

My friend, Karen Davis from my old neighborhood was also attending Mountain View. Over the years we kept in touch, but she had never mentioned that she was applying to Mountain View. Karen said she wanted to wait to see the look on my face.

Her room was down the hall from mine. We stayed up almost all night catching up on the events of our lives. Karen shared that she wasn't dating anyone at this time. I told her about my reaction when I saw Derek at the airport. Karen asked me if I was going to pursue these new feelings toward him. I told her I wasn't sure because this was unknown territory for me. She suggested that I take it one day at a time and see what happens. I agreed with her.

Chapter 5 : Secrets Exposed

My academic scholarship covered everything except my supplies and dorm room. I used money from my college savings account for what I needed. I had enrolled in general studies classes as well as some unconventional courses. One of the courses was photography. I had so many pictures from that summer. I also had an assigned dorm mate, but for some reason, she dropped out at the last minute. I used the extra bed as my workstation.

I enjoyed being at college. I had a tremendous hunger for learning. I went to as many lectures that I could fit into my schedule. I hung on to every word that my professors spoke. I was captivated by the college atmosphere. I even had early morning classes. Since I had a full schedule, Karen and I would hang out sometimes after homework and often on Saturdays.

Derek worked part-time at the campus bookstore. He was saving up money to buy a car. He worked Mondays, Wednesdays, and Fridays. The bookstore was closed on Sundays. On Sundays, we would spend time together sightseeing.

I loved the fact that Mountain View College was indeed on top of a picturesque mountain. We also found a theatre that had an Alfred Hitchcock movie marathon in the nearby town. During spring break, I went home to see my mother. Derek stayed at Mountain View.

My mother was thrilled to see me because she had some big news to share. David Williams and she were engaged and the wedding would be during the summer. I was truly happy for her. She was going to keep her house so that I would have a place to crash whenever I came home and because she didn't want to move her dental practice.

The months went by so fast. Summer was finally here and the rehearsal dinner was two nights before my mother's wedding. It was catered by my mother's and Mr. Williams' favorite restaurant. I was seated next to Mr. William's best friend, Carlton Williams. He was a judge and the wedding officiant.

Mr. Williams' and Judge Carlton's personalities were contrary to each other. Mr. Williams was quiet and conservative; Judge Carlton was loud and outspoken. Since they had the same last name, they were asked if they were brothers. They both were at the top of their class at Harvard and were very competitive. Judge Carlton said, "I always spoke up and said that Dave was my brother by another mother!" He burst out in laughter.

Judge Carlton was from Pittsburgh, Pennsylvania, where he grew up in the inner city. He had one of those personalities where you felt like you knew him for years. Judge Carlton was married to his third wife, but he had no children.

David Williams was the middle child of a privileged family who moved from Washington, D.C. to Rockville, Maryland when he was in high school. He had never been married and had no children. Mr. Williams had an older brother and younger sister. Both of his parents and his brother were judges. His sister recently graduated from Harvard. After college, it was expected that Mr. Williams would work at a large law firm and then seek a judgeship. After passing the bar examination, Mr. Williams decided to open up his own law firm because he didn't want to follow the pattern of his parents and brother.

When Mr. Williams introduced my mother and me to his family, we both felt the friction. They were not what I expected his family to be like. They carried a sense of arrogance with their

Chapter 5 : Secrets Exposed

expensive clothes and mannerisms. I don't know about my mother, but I felt uncomfortable around them.

The rehearsal dinner was a reunion with my mother's side of the family. I met my Grandmother Louise, uncles, and aunts for the first time. The Rowell family was the complete opposite of the Williams. They all wore their Sunday best as if ready to attend church. Grandma Louise had on a large flowery hat. My aunts wore hats too, but not as big. From all of the information I had received about my grandmother, I was expecting a confrontation. I saw my mother and grandmother alone for few minutes before the salads were served. Then Grandma Louise hugged my mother.

Mr. Williams escorted grandmother to the table. As they were walking, she asked Mr. Williams if my mother was pregnant. He kissed her hand and said, no, then he whispered in her ear that his parents told him to wait until the wedding night to do the nasty. Grandma's mouth dropped open and my mother laughed.

My uncles Matthew and Thomas were hilarious. They told several stories of their childhood. My aunts Hannah and Sarah would often intrude into their stories to make corrections. The Williams didn't participate in any conversations except among themselves. During the dinner, I went to the bathroom and Mrs. Williams and her daughter came into the room. They didn't know I was in there also.

They were making sarcastic remarks about my family's jargon and clothes. When they started making distasteful remarks about my mother, I came busting out of the bathroom stall. They both cringed when they saw me. I gave them the most menacing look that I could make, washed my hands, and left. When they finally came back to the dinner table, I gave a subtle look at them. My intent was to let them know I had a unique position over the situation. I didn't want to spoil the wedding, so I didn't tell my mother until a few months later about the bathroom incident. She told me that Mr. Williams had warned her that they were distasteful. My mother thought that their opinions were insignificant to her life.

Mr. Williams had a big house and a large backyard. The small wedding service was held there. It was just the two families and a few close friends. I was the maid of honor and Mr. Williams' brother was the best man. My mother's oldest brother had walked her down the aisle. I had never seen my mother so happy. It was a beautiful day. They had a short honeymoon because Mr. Williams had a big law case to prepare for.

When I arrived back at college, Derek announced that he was the assistant manager for the bookstore. He had designed a computer program to upgrade the bookstore. Students would be able to order their books in advance and then pick them up later. His program also made it easier to run the bookstore. Derek and the store manager were able to split workdays. The manager would work Monday through Friday 8:00 a.m. to 12:00 p.m. Derek would work Monday through Friday 12:00 p.m. to 4:00 p.m. They would alternate working on Saturdays. The college was also very impressed with Derek's work and gave him a cash bonus large enough that he was able to buy a new car instead of a used one.

I didn't see him much during the first few months when classes started in the fall. Derek had to train Eddie Haynes, a new employee. Eddie had been kicked out of several boarding schools. He worked at the bookstore because his father had cut him off financially. The money earned at the bookstore wasn't enough for Eddie, so he started gambling. Karen mentioned to me that rumors were going around campus that Derek and Eddie were sexually involved. I told her that the next time Derek and I got together, I would most certainly ask him about Eddie.

Derek and I went to a movie marathon the following Sunday. I told him about the rumors going around about him and Eddie. Derek scolded me for listening to rumors. He asked if I had forgotten about our last year of high school. I knew that he was referring to the trouble caused by Amber Greene's rumors.

"Ray, you know firsthand what rumors did to you and Mr. Jackson."

"I didn't say that I believed the rumors, Derek."

"Eddie has left town, so there's no more reason for anyone to talk anymore."

"So why did he leave town?" I asked.

"Eddie got expelled."

"Why did he get expelled?"

"He was running a poker game on campus."

"I thought there was no gambling allowed on campus."

"Well, that's one reason why he got expelled. Someone who lost a lot of money at a game snitched. Eddie found out who snitched, he made threats. Eddie's father is Judge Roger Haynes, who is campaigning for re-election. So before the press found out the whole story, his father pulled some strings, made some bribes, and sent Eddie to Europe to live with his mother."

"Eddie's mother is an actress there. So now do you see? How could I be in a relationship with someone like Eddie? Eddie has a wicked charisma that some people are attracted to. I'm not." Hearing his words, I apologized to Derek and nothing more was said about Eddie.

We started our old routine again. One Sunday, as we were watching a movie, a scary part played and I almost jumped into Derek's lap. That was when we had our very first passionate kiss. After that, we started holding hands everywhere we went. If we didn't have a class or he wasn't at the bookstore, we were together.

In town, Derek found a new seafood restaurant. It was good to go to a fancy restaurant. Because of the class schedule I had, I mostly ate cafeteria and vending food. We planned to go again the Sunday before Christmas break.

Karen and I had gone out on Saturday and gotten our hair done. We also treated ourselves to a manicure and pedicure. While shopping, I had bought a new dress and matching shoes. When I opened my dorm door for Derek, he was speechless.

After dinner, the unexpected happened. Derek took out a little black box. When he opened it, inside was the most beautiful ring I had ever seen. He got down on one knee and asked me to marry him. It was like a scene from one of the movies we had watched. I said, "Yes!"

When I went home for Christmas break, I told my mother about Derek and me. She had some news also. She was two months pregnant! My mother was praying that it would be a girl. So we both were excited about all this good news. We set the date for my wedding the weekend before my birthday in June. My mother insisted on having a big wedding. I could not deprive her of that precious moment.

I asked Mr. Williams if he would escort me down the aisle.

"I will walk you down the aisle on one condition."

"What is that?"

"Stop calling me Mr. Williams and start calling me Dave."

"Dave, would you please escort me down the aisle?"

"That would be my pleasure and honor."

My mother just sat and cried. She was so emotional, I don't know if it was because she was pregnant or not.

Every other weekend for five months, if I didn't have any big school assignments, I would catch the train back home to plan the wedding with my mother. It was a lot of work. As we started getting closer to June, I had started having doubts about getting married. I called Aunt Lottie and asked her, "Do you think that we are too young to get married?"

"Ray," she replied, "you are older than when your Uncle Claude and I got married. Look how long you have known Derek. Do you really love him?"

I answered, "Yes."

"Does he really love you?"

"Yes."

"Then that's all that really matters." As always, her words made me feel so much better.

It was at the wedding rehearsal dinner that I met the rest of Derek's family for the first time. His mother had two sisters, Ethel and Jean. Ethel had five daughters, three of them were in our wedding party. During the rehearsal dinner, I felt like everyone was staring at me and whispering. It made me a little uncomfortable.

Jean came and sat beside me. She started asking me different questions like, "How did Derek and you meet? How long did you date?" I felt like I was being interrogated by the police.

Jean was very talkative and didn't give me time to answer one question before she fired off another one. Suddenly, she asked me a strange question. "Have you met Derek's friend, Eddie?"

"No, he has been out of town for the past year."

"I was so surprised when the news came out that Derek was marrying a girl. Derek had been a momma's boy after his father was killed during the war. He cried every time his mother left him. Derek was always a child who stayed to himself. The entire family is so glad he grew out of that state and found a woman to marry."

Her sister, Ethel told her, "You shouldn't be reliving Derek's past with his future wife."

"Well, everyone in the family thought he was a momma's boy but didn't have the nerve to say it." Jean snapped back at her.

Then Ethel snapped back, reminding her that he was a child who had lost his father. I thought this was a very awkward conversation to have with someone they had just met. I had heard enough so I made an excuse that I needed to check on my pregnant mother to get away from them.

We got married at Aunt Lottie's former church. All my family from Louisiana came to the wedding except my two half-brothers. I wore a beautiful white satin dress. My bouquet had white tulips with a lily in the center. Derek's oldest cousin, Liz, was my matron of honor. My best friend, Karen was my maid of honor. Sharon, my cousins, Alfrieda and Georgia, and Derek's two other cousins, Karla and Chloe, were bridesmaids. I also had two flower girls, a ring bearer, and a bell ringer.

All of the women in the bridal party wore lilac dresses. Their bouquets were made of lilacs with baby's breath surrounding them. Derek wore a white tuxedo. Derek's mentor, Mr. Cooper, was his best man. Karla and Chloe had their husbands as groomsmen. Sharon, Alfrieda, and Georgia were escorted by three of Derek's chess buddies. The best man, groomsmen, ring bearer, bell ringer, and ushers all wore black suits with lilac bowties, cummerbunds, and boutonnieres.

Dave and my mother gave us a cruise as a wedding present. I didn't want to go on a cruise because I didn't want to miss the birth of my sister. My mother insisted that she would not have her while we were gone. My mother was right and she gave birth to my little sister, Krystal Renee, on July fourth.

Dave suggested that we go somewhere close for our honeymoon and go on the cruise for our first anniversary. Derek and I agreed to go to New York for our honeymoon. During the train ride to New York, I couldn't stop thinking about the conversation that I had with Derek's aunts. I didn't share this conversation with

Derek or anyone else, however, it left me with some doubts. Did I really know Derek?

Once we got to our hotel suite, we had such a good time and I soon forgot about those doubts. We saw Broadway plays, did some shopping, and went sightseeing.

What made our marriage so wonderful was that we were already best friends. We didn't have to learn about each other like most couples. I had always said I wanted to marry a man like Uncle Claude, so I did.

Derek always left little love notes around our place. He held the door open and pulled my chair out for me when I sat down to eat. Derek was very gentle and passionate with me during our lovemaking. He knew the horror of my past and was always considerate of that.

We found a small furnished apartment off-campus. The rent fit our budget. Derek didn't like the furniture so we went looking for slipcovers, pillows, rugs, and lamps. He seemed to have a knack for decorating. We didn't have to buy any appliances because there were so many among our wedding presents.

Derek did most of the cooking. I cleaned after and washed the dishes. I really didn't have much to clean because he would wash his pots and pans as he cooked. We also used plastic utensils and paper plates to eat with during the week. This was a perfect partnership. We had a routine once we came home from our classes and his job. First dinner, then our homework, clean, and the finale was intimacy.

Chapter 5 : Secrets Exposed

After a few months, I saw that Derek was a compulsive cleaner. He would constantly clean up behind me. I was borderline messy. He said everything had to be in its proper place. Most women would appreciate a man that cleans, but it was just too compulsive to me. I spoke to my mother about Derek's compulsive cleaning.

My mother thought that was minor to the fact that Dave snored and had smelly feet. Often, she had to turn the baby monitor up real loud to drown out his snoring. My mother explained that nasal strips helped with his snoring. She hadn't found a remedy for his smelly feet, so she just kept a lot of clean socks and odor eaters for him.

We started reminiscing back to the days when Derek would cook on the weekends. My mother and I would tease Derek that if Ms. Bowman should ever quit, he could have her job. The kitchen would be spotless. Then I remembered that every semester he had a different dorm mate. All had complained that Derek acted too much like their mother. I didn't give it much thought back then. I guess it was because I didn't live with him every day.

By winter break, I had forced myself to get used to his cleaning habits, but another pattern of behavior started a year later. He started staying out late. Because I am a sound sleeper, at first I didn't notice what time he came home. I wasn't concerned until I found out that Eddie was back in town. It was then that I started having real suspicions that some shenanigans were going on between Derek and Eddie.

I spoke to Karen about this. She suggested that Derek invite Eddie over for dinner and that she would come also. The whole week leading up to Sunday's dinner, Derek seemed so distant.

Anytime I entered a room that he was in, he would leave. I would try to discuss what to cook and he would just shrug his shoulders.

The night of the dinner, Eddie did not start the night off right. He was thirty minutes late. He kept apologizing but his words didn't seem to be sincere. The whole night he kept flirting with Karen. Derek seemed a little upset about the flirtation. In between flirts, Eddie would ask questions about me and Derek. Then it was my turn to ask questions about him.

"Eddie, how was Europe?"

"Oh, I just loved it," he said. "You have so much freedom to be yourself over there. The only thing that I missed over here was the food. My mother doesn't have domestic help, so I ate out a lot."

"Do you regret coming back to Mountain View?"

"Well, I did miss my friends," he replied, and he looked straight at Derek. Derek quickly put his head down.

"My father won his re-election and my expulsion was over, so that's why I came back. When I heard the news about your marriage, I was dying to meet you."

Just at that moment, Derek jumped up and yelled, "Dessert anyone?"

Eddie commented to Derek, "I hope you made my favorite dessert."

Eddie volunteered to drive Karen back to her dorm. Derek was very quiet as we cleaned up. Then he lashed out at me. I didn't understand why Derek was so furious. He started calling Karen awful names.

I asked him, "Why are so mad? Eddie is your friend. Karen is my friend. I was hoping we all could be friends. I felt this dinner would be an opportunity to learn a little more about Eddie." Derek could not explain why he was so angry with me.

"Why are you being so protective toward Eddie?" I asked. I couldn't believe our first argument was about someone who was a total stranger to me.

"I'm not being protective!" Derek shouted as he stormed out of the apartment. I had never seen that side of him. I was still cleaning when Derek came back. He started kissing me on the back of my neck. Then I smelled alcohol.

"Have you been drinking?"

"Just a little bit," he replied.

That night, when we made love it was very different. Usually Derek is so passionate and gentle. But tonight he was forceful and rough. He did and said things that were totally out of his character.

He asked me afterward, "Did you like it?" I lied and said yes. This was the first time I had ever lied to him. I promised myself if he ever acted like that again, I was going to tell him the truth.

The next day, I asked Karen what she thought of Eddie. She said, "When he drove me back to the dorm, he tried to come upstairs with me. Then he suggested going off-campus to a motel. I told him I'm waiting for love."

Eddie had been charming by holding doors and holding out the chairs. Karen said he didn't mention anything about the dinner.

After that night, I would often see Derek following Eddie around, trying to talk to him. But it was obvious Eddie was ignoring Derek. Sometimes, Derek would be on the phone and, as soon as I entered the room, he would hang up. There was a cold, uneasy feeling deep within the pit of my stomach.

The summer before graduation, I went home for Krystal's second birthday party. Karen rode with me because she hadn't seen her mother and sister in a while. It was Derek's Saturday to work and he said that there was inventory to do the next day. I was happy that Karen wanted to ride with me. We skipped classes and left that Friday.

I had been so preoccupied with the change in Derek's behavior that I forgot to make a doctor's appointment. I had been on birth control since starting my menstrual cycle. My cycle was so abnormal. There had been times that I had gone two months without a period at all. Recently, I told the doctor, "I think I need a higher dosage of birth control pills or a different brand because I haven't had a period for the past three months." She asked, "Do you have any other concerns?" I told her, "I have been feeling dizzy and nauseated."

The doctor asked why I waited so long for her. I told her I had a lot of personal issues and I just didn't make the time. She told me that the procedure was to take a pregnancy test first. The pregnancy test came back positive.

My doctor gave me a sonogram and printed the picture of our baby. I couldn't stop looking at the little feet and hands. I was scared and excited that I was pregnant. She told me, "It is time to think of the baby now and take better care of yourself." She handed me some pamphlets and told me to make another appointment for next month.

My mother threw a princess-themed birthday party for Krystal. There was a little riding train, a moon bounce, face painting, and everyone was dressed as royalty. As I watched the kids playing, I just imagined myself with a child. I thought about having a little girl or maybe twins. I wanted one boy and one girl.

Then I thought about names. If I had a girl, her first name would be Josephine after my father. Her middle name would be Ella after my favorite singer, Ella Fitzgerald. The boy's name would be Joseph James. My mother was too busy for me to tell her about my pregnancy.

Karen and I went back to Mountain View early on Sunday. I told Karen the news about my pregnancy. She was thrilled. I told her I hoped that would snap Derek out of his negative mood.

After dropping Karen off, I rushed home to cook dinner before Derek got there. I just couldn't believe that I was three months pregnant. I knew I had gained weight but I had thought that it was because I was eating out more.

I drove up to the apartment and saw Derek's car there. I thought to myself, *he sure is home early*. I was still thinking about how I was going to tell Derek the news. As I walked through the front door I heard laughter coming from the bedroom.

Voices from the bedroom snapped me out of my daydream. I knew one voice was Derck's. I walked slowly toward the bedroom. I thought *this can't be right*. I recognized the second voice as Eddie's.

My heart was beating so fast. I burst into the bedroom and to my horror, right in front of me was my worst fear. Derek and Eddie were naked in bed together! Derek was startled and turned around toward me. I started feeling sick to my stomach and light-headed.

I ran toward the kitchen and began throwing up in the sink. I don't know if it was from my emotional dilemma or the pregnancy. I stopped throwing up after a couple of minutes. A whole volcano of emotions started boiling up—betrayal, abandonment, numbness, unforgiveness, revenge, and stupidity. For the first time, I really wanted to commit murder.

Derek came out with a robe on and tried to explain. I was so distraught, I didn't hear a thing that he was saying. I slapped his face three times. I had never been violent toward him before. I screamed at him, "Don't come near me!" I ran toward the front door. Eddie was in the hallway with a smirk on his face.

I left the apartment and got in my car with tears flowing. Here I was ecstatic to come home and tell my husband that we were going to have a baby. I knew we had agreed to wait until we graduated from college. I snapped out of me reliving the past few hours when Derek touched my shoulder. I told him again, "Don't touch me." Then I drove away. I didn't call Karen or anyone. I just wanted to be alone.

I was too tired to drive back to D.C., so I drove into town and checked into a motel until the next day. Since we lived near a small town, there was only one motel. Derek lied to the motel manager to find out the room I was in and he started calling my room phone. When I answered the phone and heard his voice, I knocked the phone off the nightstand and the TV remote fell too. The television then came on and a man was preaching about hope.

I listened to him and then looked for the Gideon Bible, which is usually available in most motel rooms. I followed him as he gave scriptures about having hope in God:

- Psalm 25:2; 33:18; 39:7; 42:5; 119:49–50
- Proverbs 10:28
- Jeremiah 29:11
- Romans 8:24–25; 15:4; 15:13
- Hebrews 11:1

This pastor was saying everything I was feeling. It seemed like he was talking directly to me. The last scripture mentioned was Psalms 91. He encouraged everyone to recite Psalms 91 as a personal prayer, inserting our own name as we recite it. After the pastor went off the air, I keep reading the scriptures over and over until I fell asleep.

I was awakened at 1:00 a.m. because of banging on my motel door. I got out of bed, looked through the peephole, and saw it was Derek. I could tell that he was drunk again.

Someone called the sheriff and they arrived to quiet him down. He was slurring his words as he told them that his wife was inside the room and that I wouldn't let him in. The deputy walked Derek over to the police car.

The sheriff knocked on the door and asked if he could talk with me. I told the sheriff that I didn't want to see my husband because I had caught him in the act of infidelity. He asked me if I wanted to file charges against him for harassing me. "No, just make him leave," I said. The sheriff told me good night and left.

The sheriff then walked back to the police car where they had Derek in the back seat. I overheard the deputy tell Derek that they would give him a ride home because they would not let him drive drunk. I didn't know that my path with the sheriff would soon cross again.

When I stepped out the motel door the next morning, I didn't see Derek. He was behind the door and startled me. He tried to apologize, but I didn't want to hear anything he had to say. I started backing away from him, but I didn't realize that I was backing toward the steps. I lost my balance and fell down the steps.

When I woke up, I was in the hospital. My mother was asleep in a chair by my bed. I could see that Dave was outside the hospital door sitting in a chair. My mother felt me moving in the bed and opened her eyes.

"What happened?" I asked.

She told me, "You fell down the motel steps and Derek called an ambulance. Why were you at a motel?"

I recounted everything that had happened to me within the last forty-eight hours. She burst into tears. My mother climbed into the hospital bed with me and hugged me.

"I'm so sorry that you went through everything alone."

Chapter 5 : Secrets Exposed

"All that matters is that you and Dave are here now." The doctor on call stepped into the hospital room. I didn't like the look on her face.

"Mrs. Frazer, it is my deepest regret to tell you that you had a miscarriage." I felt crushed and started crying uncontrollably. My mother held me tight and cried with me.

Wednesday morning, after being released from the hospital, my mother drove me back to their house. Dave was there waiting on us. He hugged me and said how sorry he was for me and that this was my home also. I thanked him.

I took a long hot shower and went to bed. I felt like the weight of the world had been placed upon my shoulders. I slept for a whole day. My mother finally woke me up so I could eat. I told her that I wasn't hungry.

We had a small memorial service for Josephine Ella. After a couple of months of resting, I decided to go back to college to finish my degree. I was determined not to run and hide anymore. I wanted to accelerate my class schedule to get my degree faster. Dave handled my divorce and canceled the apartment lease. Derek never knew I was pregnant. I wanted to put as much distance from Derek, Eddie, and Pennsylvania as quickly as possible.

When I finally graduated, the plan was for my mother to catch a flight to Pennsylvania and we would drive back to D.C. with all my things. I had just sealed the last box and took off my headphones when I heard a lot of commotion in the halls. I hadn't heard all the emergency vehicles arrive at the campus bookstore. I decided to go see what was going on.

As I approached the bookstore, I overheard the store manager give her statement to the sheriff's deputy. The store manager said that Derek and Eddie were in the backroom arguing. Derek was accusing Eddie of cheating on him. Eddie of course was denying it. The last thing she heard Derek say was "you cost me my wife, the most important person in my life. All you have ever done was to manipulate and used people for your own selfish needs." Then she heard two gunshots. Derek shot Eddie and then shot himself.

I fell to my knees and started crying. Even though Derek had hurt me so badly, I still loved him. I couldn't help but think about his mother and the baby. The sheriff that I had met that morning at the motel saw me. He ran over to where I was. The sheriff thought I was going to pass out. He held me until my mother found me and took me away from the store.

We got in my car and just drove away. I found out a couple of months later that Eddie didn't die. The bullet had shattered his spine. He was paralyzed from the waist down. I thought to myself *that was good*. Eddie would be in a wheelchair for the rest of his life because of all the hurt and trouble he had caused others.

During the ride home, I replayed in my mind what the store manager had said. After catching Derek and Eddie in bed together, I had never talked to him again even though he had tried numerous times to contact me. Even at our divorce proceedings, he had tried to give me a letter. I tore it up and threw it back at him. Those two years that we were married felt like a lifetime ago. I was so in love with him, but now I hated him just as much as I loved him. But it was ironic to hear from a total stranger that Derek still cared for me. Maybe if I had given him the chance to explain, he would still be alive.

Chapter 5 : Secrets Exposed

I didn't realize I had said the last thought out loud. Suddenly, my mother stopped the car and pulled over. As she took my tear-drenched face in her hands, she said, "You must not carry the burdens of someone's actions as your fault. Ray, you did that for five years because of my choice to abandon you and your father. Derek chose to live a double life and the choice to shoot Eddie and himself. The only choice you made was to love someone with your whole heart. You gave yourself to Derek and he threw your love and trust away. So do not let this event destroy your future and your destiny. Together we are going to take it step-by-step, day-by-day."

I convinced myself to go to the funeral and be a support for Derek's mother. I could tell when I walked into the church that no one had expected to see me. It was a closed casket funeral because Derek had shot himself in the face.

His mother had his high school graduation picture blown up and upright beside his casket. The picture reminded me of the man I fell in love with. The man I was supposed to raise a family and share a life with. His mother grabbed my hand and pulled me to sit beside her. We held hands during the entire service. We gave comfort to each other. After the service, the morticians took the casket. There was a repast downstairs. His mother asked me to stay behind and let everyone else go. She wanted to talk with me.

"Raynelle," she said, "I'm so sorry about what my son did to you. I'm glad you came so I can apologize to you in person. I was going to write you a long letter once the memorial service was over."

"Why do you need to apologize?"

"Raynelle, I guess you wondered why I was surprised to find out that the two of you were getting married. The truth is Derek and I had been estranged when he became friends with Eddie. Eddie was like an evil puppet master and Derek was his stringed puppet. For some reason, Eddie had a stronghold over Derek. He had convinced Derek to stay away from me and the rest of the family."

"When you two started dating, it brought my Derek back to me. Then when you two got married I thought that his relationship with Eddie was over. Then Eddie came back to town and Derek changed back."

"Raynelle, I tried to tell Derek to talk to you. If only he had, I'm sure that you two could have gone to marriage counseling together or something. Maybe through a counselor he would have found out he did want a life with you, or Eddie, and not have all those secrets. You have no idea what I have had to live with." After all the guilt and shame Mrs. Frazer shared, I didn't want to add to her pain about the grandchild that she would never see.

As I was riding from the funeral, I kept playing the conversation that I had with Mrs. Frazer through my mind over and over again. I began to think about my little girl. I was so glad that I had the sonogram picture printed. I felt that I had made the right choice not to tell Mrs. Frazer about the miscarriage. I did tell one of her sisters about the miscarriage and told her to decide the right time to tell Mrs. Frazer. She agreed.

As time went on, I kept finding myself going into children's clothing stores and playgrounds—anywhere there were children. My mother expressed numerous times that she was concerned about me. She suggested that I seek counseling. I told her, that I would think about it. I didn't tell anyone about that night at the motel. I had made up my mind to get an abortion.

I was feeling so much pain. I felt that I would hate the baby. My mother and I had a conversation a while ago about abortion. She told me, "All children have the right to life. Unborn babies are people too. If they are allowed to live, one day they might find the cure for a disease or invent something to change the world. Children who suffer and die through the process of abortions are not forgotten. To God, each life is sacred, and He remembers and knows who they are."

In my heart, I was grieving the loss of two people—the man I married and the baby that I had carried for three months. I hadn't felt so lonely and lost since Papa's death. Oh, how I missed my Papa. Even though my mother was doing all the right things, it was something about being in my papa's arms. I felt loved and untouchable from anything that would ever hurt me again. I continually looked at the photo albums of our wedding, honeymoon, and time at college.

My mother inquired with one of her clients who was a grief minister, Dr. Woods. Dr. Woods suggested a pamphlet that gave the particular signs people displayed during grief. When my mother finished with her last client, she decided to look at the pamphlet. She discovered that I was demonstrating most of the signs listed.

Mrs. Bowman, my mother's housekeeper, went back to North Carolina shortly after my mother's wedding. Dave already had a housekeeper named Jo Ann McDaniel. I liked her a lot because she reminded me of Mrs. Bowman. They hired a nanny for Krystal named Kerry Moore. They found her through one of Dave's clients. I didn't like her very much. She was young, arrogant, and my mother was caught in the middle between the two of us. I would complain to my mother about her and she would complain to my mother about me.

One day, I took Krystal to the park without telling Kerry. Kerry became frantic and called my mother at work. My mother went into her office, looked at the camera monitors, pushed the rewind button, and saw that I had taken Krystal. My mother calmed Kerry down and told her that I had called and told her that I had Krystal. I guess that my mother lied because she didn't want Kerry to know about the hidden cameras in the house.

However, when she talked to me later she was furious. When I brought Krystal back to Kerry, she rolled her eyes at me and took Krystal to the nursery. When my mother got home, she asked me to go into the backyard so we could talk and Kerry could not hear us. My mother told me about the security cameras that Dave had put in most of the house. He had the cameras installed because he was a lawyer and there were a lot of strangers who came and did work around the house. Dave had more cameras installed when they hired Kerry.

My mother confessed that recently she had Dave install cameras in my bedroom. Now I was furious. I felt that my privacy had been violated. My mother assured me that she was the only one that monitored the cameras for my bedroom and Krystal's nursery. She thought by telling me her confession would make things better. My mother said, "I was worried about you because you were going through depression." I decided to go back to my mother's house to live.

Chapter 5 : Secrets Exposed

My mother waited a few days for me to calm down and then she approached me. "You should seek counseling with Dr. Woods." She recounted all the information that she had read. I was still a little angry with my mother about those cameras so I didn't feel like taking advice from her. However, because of my mother's persistence, I decided to go.

Dr. Woods first told me about her educational background and then the reason why she became a grief counselor. She really didn't catch my attention until she divulged her life story. It was very similar to mine. Once our appointment time was over, I told her, "I will be back."

After a few months of meeting with Dr. Woods, I started opening up to her about what I was feeling. Since Dr. Woods was a Christian counselor, she included Bible scriptures in her therapy sessions. So many of my childhood Sunday school lessons came back to my memory, especially Psalm 27. We both concluded that I hadn't really grieved after my father's tragic death. Then I was forced into an entirely different world with a mother that I really didn't know. Dr. Woods was able to help me unpack the root of all my depression.

One day unexpectedly, my mother presented me with a job offer. I knew it was her way of getting my mind off of me. Her receptionist had to leave town for a family emergency and she asked if I would fill in for her. I was reluctant at first but I said yes. Since moving back to my house, I hadn't made up my mind about what I wanted to do with the rest of my life.

Every Saturday was reserved for kids' dental appointments. I felt more comfortable with the kids than with their parents. I began to tell stories to the kids as they waited for their appointments. It really seemed to calm them down, especially the new patients. I got deeply attached to one little girl named Camille. I had the sonogram picture of my baby girl framed and kept it on the desk. One day Camille asked me about the picture.

I told her, "This was my baby girl that died."

She said, "I'm sorry that she died." Camille told me, "I know how you feel because last year my baby brother died."

I felt the conversation was getting too deep, so I changed the subject. I told Camille I really liked her name.

She smiled and said, "I like your name much better. I wish you could work here forever."

"I am just filling in temporarily."

"What is your real job?"

"I haven't decided, What do you think I should be?"

"A teacher because you tell good stories."

When I went home that night, I couldn't stop thinking about her. I thought if I ever have another little girl, I would want her to be just like Camille.

Once my mother's receptionist came back to work, I began to feel depressed again. It wasn't long afterward that a missionary position came open. My mother explained that my volunteering might fill that void in my life. She said, "the best thing anyone can do in life is to help someone else."

Chapter 5 : Secrets Exposed

I announced to my mother, "I don't want any more advice from you. I am going to Louisiana to visit Uncle Claude and Aunt Lottie."

Uncle Claude and Aunt Lottie now lived at a senior living place called Magnolia Estates. Each resident had a single-level home with two bedrooms, a kitchen, a living room, and one bathroom. On the property, there was also a recreation center and indoor pool. Six months prior to me visiting Louisiana, Aunt Lottie ran into my oldest brother, Andre, while he was visiting his girlfriend's grandmother. His girlfriend's grandfather had died and her grandmother was tired of the harsh, cold winters and hot summers in New York. Her grandmother had really missed her husband and there were too many memories. Andre had mentioned to his girlfriend about the place where his Uncle Claude and Aunt Lottie were living.

After spending a week with Aunt Lottie, she asked me, "Do you trust me? Have I ever lied to you?"

"No, Aunt Lottie" I responded, "but I do wish that you had told me about my mother when she first came back to D.C."

Aunt Lottie replied, "I didn't think that it was my place to tell you. Only your father could make that decision." she replied. "You know that he was a very prideful and stubborn man, so I had to respect his decision. He was led by his feelings and emotions when he refused to let your mother start seeing you again. I didn't agree with his decision and told him that on many occasions. We all make mistakes and need to learn from them or we are destined to relive them again and again. Some mistakes are engineered and manipulated by other people."

I knew that Aunt Lottie was going somewhere else with this conversation.

"Why are you talking about trust? Didn't I trust you, Aunt Lottie?"

With an indescribable look on her face, she said, "I have invited someone over for dinner tomorrow."

"Aunt Lottie!" I exclaimed, "I hope you are not trying to fix me up with someone because I am definitely not ready to date or even think about dating yet."

"No, Ray, I invited Andre." Immediately, I felt myself getting angry.

Sensing my emotions, she looked right into my eyes and said, "Ray, listen to me carefully. Do you remember the conversation that I had with you about why I visited the jail to see the man who had killed my son? I told you then that unforgiveness can get so rooted in our inner self that it will choke anything good out. You must know that I would never take your feelings lightly."

"I have had several long conversations with Andre. He is no longer that twelve-year-old boy anymore. With all of my being, I can truly tell you that he is remorseful for what he did to you that day and wants to apologize."

I asked with hostility in my voice, "What brought this transformation on?"

Aunt Lottie went on to tell me that Andre was a professor of music at the Albany College of Fine Arts in New York. Like my father, Andre played in a jazz band occasionally after his classes. He played the piano but felt that he didn't have the talent for it. His girlfriend, Daniella, had come to see him play one time and then she signed up for his class. Andre and Daniella both felt the attraction between the two of them. He was mesmerized the first time he saw her, but the faculty wasn't allowed to date any of the students. After classes, they would have long conversations about music and her family. They officially started dating once Daniella graduated from college.

Andre took Daniella home to New Orleans to meet his mother. She didn't approve of Daniella's looks, her family business, and that she was also a musician. Ms. Duplantier forbid Andre to ever see her again. It hurt him deep in his heart the way his mother treated Daniella. Andre has been estranged from his mother and brother ever since.

"Daniella is a strong, independent-minded young lady," Aunt Lottie said. "She reminds me a little of you."

"Have you ever met her?" I asked.

"Yes, I have. Andre feels that Daniella is the woman that he wants to marry. One day, Daniella confessed to him her deepest secret, that she was raped by her oldest brother's best friend. She had never told anyone else before. Andre now feels that he doesn't deserve her because of what he did to you."

Sarcastically, I said, "Well, he is right. If Daniella is that wonderful, Andre doesn't deserve her."

Aunt Lottie reminded me, "Ms. Duplantier had a very controlling hold over her sons. They were only young boys trying to please their mother. Both Andre and you need forgiveness in your lives. You can't change the past. You both have come through a lot of heartaches, disappointment, and hard times. You both need to start living for today!"

"Ray put your past behind you and start living for the now! None of us can change our yesterdays because they are behind us. None of us can live in our tomorrows because tomorrow never comes. You must never allow your past to determine your future. I have lived long enough on this earth to have concluded not to hold on to hatred or regrets. Don't let your past disappointments dictate your future."

Even though Aunt Lottie, as usual, displayed wisdom, I wasn't convinced to forgive Andre. However, I was intrigued to hear more about Andre's girlfriend.

Aunt Lottie said, "Her full name is Daniella Hendrix and she is a native of Macomb, New York. She has fair skin, red hair, and deep blue eyes. Daniella is unique in a lot of ways."

Aunt Lottie asked me, "Did you know that only 1% of redheads have blue eyes?"

"No."

"The rest of her family has brown eyes. Daniella's family owns one of the largest, dairy farms in the state of New York. Daniella also is a twin like Andre; her twin brother's name is Dan. Dan and Daniella are prodigies. She plays classical piano and he plays the violin. Dan and Daniella were born two months premature. The doctors hadn't thought that they would survive, but they proved everyone wrong. They were fighters. They both were sick a lot during their early childhood years."

Aunt Lottie continued to tell me that their mom had found among some old videotapes of a cartoon called Super Friends. There was a brother and sister team called the wonder twins on that show. The wonder twins were vulnerable separately, but together they were invincible. Mrs. Hendrix had a friend who made costume jewelry to make Dan and Daniella rings with two halves that fit together to make one ring. In school, they took being the wonder twins to heart by becoming bullies. The school administration started putting them in separate classes.

They were teased a lot because they were smaller than most kids and had red hair. It was when they started playing music that their talents were discovered. They received full scholarships to the Albany College of Fine Arts. Dan and Daniella had inherited their musical talents from their mother, who used to be an opera singer. Their mother had sung professionally until deciding to give up her career to get married and start a family. They have two older brothers named Aiden and Ryan. Daniella is the only daughter.

Aunt Lottie's facial expression became solemn as she told me Daniella's rape story. "Daniella's oldest brother went out drinking with his friends a lot. One day, his best friend, Jeff, was drunk and found Daniella working in their barn alone. He started talking to Daniella, telling her how pretty she was. Jeff said in an alarming statement that he had never had sex with a redhead. He wondered was the hair over her entire body was red. Daniella tried to leave the barn, but he kept blocking the way."

"She told Jeff that Dan was on the way. He knew that it was a lie because Aiden had told him earlier Dan was sick. He started rubbing on her and she pushed his hands away. Daniella saw a pitchfork, but Jeff blocked the way before she could reach it. He was twice her size and, just when she was about to yell, he placed his enormous hand over her mouth. Jeff pushed her down with his other hand and raped her. After he was done he yelled at Daniella that no one would believe her if she told anybody. Then Jeff started crying and saying that her brothers would kill him and begged her not to tell."

Aunt Lottie continued in a low voice, "Dan heard Daniella crying hysterically that night in her room. He knew something was wrong. Once Daniella confided in him what had happened, Dan blamed himself. She told him that he had the flu, so he couldn't have been there. Dan began plotting revenge against Jeff. Daniella told him to remember that things always come back to you either good or bad."

"It wasn't long before Mrs. Hendrix started seeing a difference in Daniella's personality. She would be the first to get up and do her chores so that she could avoid everyone else. Daniella stopped playing the piano and just stayed in her room. Her appetite changed, and she didn't want to be bothered with any of her brothers."

"One night, Mrs. Hendrix caught Dan sneaking out of Daniella's room. She caught Dan and asked him, 'What is wrong with Daniella?'" Dan said, "The girls at school are picking on her again."

"Mrs. Hendrix also had noticed how Dan and Daniella were whispering a lot. She asked Dan again what was wrong and he told his mother that Daniella had a crush on a boy and he was moving away. Dan had a knack for lying when it came to protecting Daniella."

"Mrs. Hendrix decided to confront Daniella one night before she went to bed. Daniella told her nothing was wrong. Mrs. Hendrix told her that she was making a doctor's appointment for her, as it was time for a checkup. Daniella pleaded with her mother not to take her to the doctor's."

"Two days later, they got the news that Jeff had been driving drunk and swerved off a cliff into the ocean. They never found his body. Mrs. Hendrix noticed that Daniella went back to her normal self after Jeff's memorial service. The day after the memorial service, Mrs. Hendrix confronted Daniella and told her, that she knew that something had happened with that boy. She tried to convince Daniella that she didn't ever have to feel that she couldn't tell her anything. Mrs. Hendrix grabbed and hugged Daniella for a very long time. Daniella still didn't tell her what had happened. She was too ashamed."

"Nowadays," Aunt Lottie added, "Daniella volunteers at the Hope is Here Ministries, which is an organization that helps women and children escape from sex trafficking and the trauma of being raped. Daniella became a volunteer for the Hope is Here Ministries seeking to make a difference in these women's lives. Daniella knows she had Dan to help her get through, but many other women and young girls don't have anyone to turn to. Her rape was a one-time incident, but many of these women and girls were living this trauma every day."

As I laid in bed that night, I began thinking about that entire conversation with Aunt Lottie. She is the wisest woman that I have ever known. I knew that she was right. I started thinking back to my father's viewing before the funeral. I had gone inside the church to talk to him alone. There was a young man already at the casket crying. He was there for a long while, and then another young man came in and stood beside him.

"Andre," the young man called him, "mother is looking for you." My mouth dropped open when I realized these were my two half-brothers. Quickly, I hid between the pews before they could see me. At the repast, Andre's eyes and my eyes had met once. His lips had formed words that I could not figure out. Just when he began to walk towards me, Ms. Duplantier intervened and the three of them left.

I just couldn't fall to sleep, so I got out of bed and started reading the twenty letters Aunt Lottie had given me from Andre. She said, "Andre had been writing to me for years, but he didn't have the courage to mail them." Andre had told her it was the death of our father when he started having deep remorse.

Aunt Lottie said, "You should read the letters and then decide whether to accept his apology or not." After reading the letters, my eyes were red from crying. I knew then that I had to mentally prepare myself to meet my brother again. I also remembered a session I had with Dr. Woods when we discussed that forgiveness is an important part of healing.

The following day, Uncle Claude answered the door when Andre rang the doorbell. It was hard at first to be in the same room with Andre. At twelve, he hadn't looked like my father, but now he looked just like him. He was tall, skinny, and had the same manner of speaking. He had brought Aunt Lottie some flowers and gave Uncle Claude a jazz tape that one of his students had made. Andre also had a wrapped package for me.

When I opened the package, I was surprised, even stunned. It was a framed picture of my father and me when I was three years old. My father used to take me to the Baltimore harbor to see the boats. I had my favorite sailor dress on with a matching hat. Aunt Lottie had found a captain's hat for Papa to wear whenever we went to the harbor. I had forgotten all about this until I saw the picture.

I asked Andre, "Where did you get this picture?"

He explained, "Years ago, I had asked our father to send me a picture of my little sister. This is the picture that he sent me. I found it when I was packing to go to college." Because of this little gesture, I began to feel comfortable around Andre.

After dinner, Andre asked, "Could we speak alone?" I was sensing an awkward moment between us but followed him into another room.

He looked directly into my face and said, "Raynelle, I know I have no right to ask, but would you one day in your heart please forgive me? I sincerely apologize for all the pain, hurt, and suffering that I have caused you."

"I will try, but I need a little more time. Aunt Lottie made me realize that your mother had a controlling hold on you and Alston. It's your mother that really needs to apologize to me." Andre and I never mentioned this conversation ever again.

Biblical Characters For Chapter Five

"Now, Lord, what do I wait for? My Hope is in You."
   -Psalm 39:7

David Williams And Boaz

For David Williams, Hope was in his having a relationship with Lauretta. The Bible gives the account of Boaz who had similar life events as David (in Ruth 2:1–4:13).

David and Boaz both demonstrated the characteristics of a good husband. They were both hard-working businessmen, cared for others, and provided for their families.

The Story of Boaz

Boaz was a wealthy and honorable landowner in Bethlehem from the tribe of Judah. He was a man of faith who was capable, wise, and kind. When Boaz discovered Ruth (the widow of his relative Elimelech) in his fields picking up after the reapers, he welcomed her and praised Ruth for her devotion to her mother-in-law, Naomi.

Boaz instructed his servants to take care of Ruth. Sometime later, Naomi urged Ruth to find a husband and she helped Ruth present herself to Boaz. Flattered by her humble trust, Boaz followed local Israelite customs and discussed Ruth's marital status with her closest male relative. Ruth's relative declined to marry her, so Boaz married Ruth and claimed responsibility for the property of Elimelech, who was the deceased husband of

Naomi and father-in-law of Ruth. Through their son Obed, Boaz and Ruth become ancestors of King David and The Lord Jesus Christ.

> "The wicked is driven away in his wickedness, but the righteous has Hope in his death."
> -Proverbs 14:32

Derek And Lot

Derek Frazer found Hope in himself to make life decisions. The Bible gives the account of Lot, who had similar life events as Derek (in Genesis 11:31; 12:4–5; 13:1–14 and 19:1–36).

Derek and Lot both made decisions in life with no consideration for the consequences it would have on their families. Derek's life decisions led to divorce, the loss of a child, Eddie's disability, and finally taking his own life. Lot's life decisions led to the separation of his family, the death of his wife, and incest.

The Story of Lot

Abraham's nephew, Lot, accompanied him from Mesopotamia to their final destination of Bethel. Both Lot and Abraham had large herds of cattle and their herdsmen quarreled over their pasturelands. At Abraham's suggestion, the two decided to separate.

Abraham gave Lot his choice of land. Lot chose the more fertile, well-watered site the Jordan River valley as opposed to the rocky hill country. Lot's character is revealed by the major decisions he made throughout his life. For example, he chose to pitch his tent with the worldly Sodomites, seeking riches and a life of ease rather than a path of obedience to God.

Failing to take into account the character of Sodom and Gomorrah inhabitants, Lot separated himself from Abraham's godly influence. Instead, he pursued the comforts and customs of the wicked city of Sodom. Against God's will, Lot soon was sitting in the gateway as an elder of that sinful city.

Lot was visited by two angels who warned him of God's plan to destroy that sinful city and told him he must flee or be destroyed. For associating with such sinners, Lot paid dearly with the loss of his goods and his family. When Lot was told to flee the condemned Sodom without looking back, his wife looked back anyway and God turned her into a pillar of salt.

Our Lord Jesus warned us, "Remember Lot's wife." This is a reminder of the disastrous results of disobedience. Eventually, Lot and his descendants settled in the mountainous land of Moab.

> "If I have made gold my Hope, or have said to the fine gold, 'You are my confidence'; if I rejoiced because my wealth was great, and because my hand had gained much."
> -Job 31:24–25

Eddie Haynes And Judas Iscariot

Eddie Haynes' Hope was in himself because he was a betrayer and manipulator. The Bible gives the account of Judas who had similar life events as Eddie (in Matthew 26:14–25, 47–50; 27:3–10; Mark 14:10–11, 17–21, 43–45; Luke 22:3–6, 21–23, 47–48; and John 12:4–6; 18:2–5).

Eddie and Judas were men who only cared about their selfish desires. Eddie came from a privileged family, but instead of using this advantage to help others, he lied, cheated, and belittled those around him.

Judas was in a position of privilege as one of Jesus' twelve disciples. He was also entrusted as the treasurer but he was stealing. Eddie and Judas' life choices led to a future they did not anticipate. Eddie remained disabled for the rest of his life. Judas committed suicide.

The Story of Judas

Few names in history carry the shame like the name Judas Iscariot. Judas was one of the twelve disciples. The New Testament records little except that he was not Galilean.

In his gospel, John calls Judas a thief and, along with Mark, he records that Judas criticized Mary of Bethany for anointing Jesus' feet with costly ointment. The remaining references describe his treachery and death.

It must be assumed that Jesus saw promise in Judas or he would not have called him to be a disciple. Judas' name appears in three of the lists of the disciples. Although his name always appears last, Judas must have been an important disciple because he served as their treasurer.

On the Passover night before his death, Jesus washed all the disciples' feet including Judas', yet predicted one of them would betray him. The Gospel of John clearly indicates Jesus knew the betrayer was Judas. Late that night, Judas contacted the chief priests and led the temple guards to the garden of Gethsemane.

There, in an act that deeply saddened Jesus, he identified his master with a kiss of greeting.

It is difficult to understand why Judas betrayed Jesus. Since he had access to the disciples' treasury, it seems unlikely that he did it for the money only, and thirty pieces of silver is a relatively small amount. Some have suggested that Judas thought that his betrayal would force Jesus into asserting his true power and overthrowing the Romans. Others have suggested that Judas might have become convinced that Jesus was a false Messiah and that the true Messiah was yet to come. Possibly, he was upset over Jesus' apparent indifference to the law, his association with sinners, and his violation of the Sabbath. Whatever the reason, Judas' motive remains a mystery.

Matthew reports that realizing what he had done, Judas attempted to return the money to the priests. When the priests refused to take it, Judas threw the money on the temple floor, went out, and hanged himself. Unwilling to use blood money for the temple, the priests bought a potter's field, which became known as the field of blood.

> "For we are saved through Hope, but Hope that is seen is not Hope, for why does a man still Hope for what he sees? But if we Hope for what we do not see, we wait for it with patience."
> -Romans 8:24–25

Andre and Absalom

Andre Duplantier found Hope in a chance for reconciliation with Raynelle. The Bible gives the account of Absalom who had similar life events as Andre (in 2 Samuel chapters 13–17 and 18:1-18).

Andre and Absalom were older brothers that were expected to watch over their younger siblings. Andre, unlike Absalom, had his sister's best interest when trying to reconcile. Andre showed remorse and love.

Absalom only sought revenge for Tamar. When we seek revenge, it can only have a negative outcome. God says vengeance is His only.

The Story of Absalom

Absalom was the son of King David. His half-brother, Amnon, raped their sister Tamar. King David failed to punish his oldest son, Amnon, for the rape of his half-sister Tamar. However, Absalom's advice for her to hold her peace and not to take this thing to heart showed how little Absalom understood how devastating the rape was to Tamar.

Rape is not something any woman can or should simply shrug off. Clearly, Absalom was not thinking of his sister's welfare but of how he might take revenge on Amnon. It served Absalom's purpose to have Tamar remain silent, but it did not serve Tamar's needs.

Absalom took matters into his own hands. He lured his older half-brother Amnon to his death two years later.

Chapter 6

Second Chance For Love

I stayed another week in Louisiana and then I went home. I had invited my mother to the house for a meal, so we could sit down and talk. I knew that it was time for me to forgive her also.

I shared with her all that had transpired between Andre and me. She was glad that things were better with at least one brother. She said, "I'm sure this would have made your father happy." I totally agreed with her.

A month later, Andre arranged a meeting with Daniella's parents to ask permission to marry her. He knew that Mr. and Mrs. Hendrix were traditional. They welcomed him with open arms. Mrs. Hendrix was especially grateful since he had found Magnolia Estates for her mother. Her mother had expressed how much she liked living there. Aunt Lottie and her had become the best of friends.

Andre asked Mrs. Hendrix if she would go with him to pick out the engagement ring. She left the room. Mr. Hendrix and Andre were thinking that she didn't want them to see her cry. Suddenly, she came back into the room with a small red velvet bag. Inside the bag was her mother's wedding ring. She told Andre, "I want Daniella to have it for her wedding because Daniella always admired it."

Andre said, "It will be an honor and pleasure to use her mother's ring."

Chapter 6 : Second Chance For Love

On the one-year anniversary of Andre and Daniella dating, Andre had made a dinner reservation at his friend's restaurant. Right after dinner, he excused himself from the table. Daniella was busy looking at the dessert menu when she heard a voice singing that she recognized. Andre had written her a song, *My Daniella.*

Everyone in the restaurant began to notice him. After Andre sang the last verse, he walked over to Daniella, knelt down on one knee, and took out the small red velvet bag with her grandmother's ring. With a loud voice he asked, "Will you marry me?" Daniella shouted and with tears in her eyes, shouted an exuberant "Yes!" There wasn't a dry eye in the entire restaurant.

The next day, Aunt Lottie called and told me, "Andre has proposed to Daniella and she has said yes. They are going to have a spring wedding next year in New York. Her parents haven't yet sold her grandparents' home yet, so the outdoor wedding will be there."

Aunt Lottie was so excited. She said the entire Young family was already making plans to attend. Mrs. Hendrix had invited the family to stay at the house with Daniella's grandmother instead of a hotel. It would be wonderful to see my aunts and cousins again.

One day, Andre called to tell me he would be in D.C. for a conference and asked if I would meet him for lunch. During the luncheon, Andre brought up his mother and brother. He confessed, "I didn't tell Daniella the real reason why I am estranged from my mother and brother." When Danielle asked him why he told her that his mother couldn't get over the fact that our father had married my mother instead of her and they were forbidden to communicate with me.

Andre stated, "I know that I am asking a lot, but will you support me with this explanation?" We both agreed that no one needed to know anything else. We also relayed our agreement to Uncle Claude, Aunt Lottie, and my mother.

Daniella wanted to invite Ms. Duplantier and Alston to the wedding. Andre told her that she shouldn't be surprised if they say no. Andre knew that his mother was going to refuse to come to the wedding. Ms. Duplantier was a very vindictive person. She was miserable and wanted everyone else to be miserable too. Daniella felt that now was a good time to find out more about Andre's mother and brother.

Andre told her, "Daniella, my mother is very manipulative, cunning, and controlling. As children, it had been our nanny who helped me and my brother mail letters to our father. Our nanny would also hide letters from our father under our pillows so my mother wouldn't find them. She didn't want me to become a musician or a teacher. She wanted me to go into politics. I refused, so now she is grooming Alston instead."

He explained, "My brother Alston depends on our mother for everything and he is not allowed to think for himself. Her dominance may have a lot have to do with Alston's stuttering problem. My mother even hired a speech therapist for him. I decided to go to New York for college, but Alston refused to leave Louisiana. I knew that he didn't want to leave our mother."

It wasn't long after the engagement announcement that Daniella and I became close friends. I had always wanted a big sister. Daniella invited me to New York to ask me to be in her wedding, I was surprised. She said, "I missed having a sister too." I was

Chapter 6 : Second Chance For Love

even allowed to be a part of the wedding planning with her and Mrs. Hendrix.

Since my mother had an outdoor wedding, I brought her wedding album to show them. I suggested the album might give them some ideas. Daniella confessed to me, "I did invite Ms. Duplantier and Alston to the wedding. Andre was right, Ms. Duplantier declined the invitation." About a week later, Ms. Duplantier wrote Daniella a letter telling her about the incident with me and my brothers. Hurt and confused, Daniella called off the wedding. She felt that she couldn't trust Andre or me.

I called Daniella and begged her to meet with me. Reluctantly, she agreed to meet. I started the conversation by apologizing.

"Since you have come into our lives, Andre and I have been able to reconcile. I don't believe in coincidence but fate."

Then Daniella showed me the letter that Ms. Duplantier had sent her. With a firm look upon her face she asked, "Please explain this."

Ms. Duplantier had evilly twisted the facts to make Andre look bad. I told Daniella the truth.

"I know what it is like to live with betrayal from someone that you love." I asked her how much did she know about my failed marriage. Daniella said, that she only knew that I had been married for two years and then my husband had committed suicide.

I told her, "It was a lot deeper and more serious than that." I shared with her the whole, ugly truth. I told Daniella that the one thing not mentioned in the letter from Ms. Duplantier was that

Andre had been a controlled twelve-year-old boy, but Derek had been a grown man. I also had brought with me some of the letters that Andre had written to me and let Daniella read them.

Then I said to Daniella, "That bitterness lasts longer than injustice. I had learned from past experiences that the real battle of life is in the mind, and it is those who forgive that become winners and not losers."

I expressed to her, "If I could forgive Andre, you should also. You will have a better future. Two wrongs never make a right." We hugged each other and ended our meeting as sisters again. Daniella called Andre and told him that she loved him and that the wedding was back on.

Daniella and Mrs. Hendrix decided that planning a big wedding was too much for them to do alone. Dan and Daniella still had several concerts to perform before the wedding, so they hired a wedding coordinator named Rachel Edwards. Rachel was smooth and ever so calm, making the whole process easy and effortless for both Daniella and Mrs. Hendrix. Her staff was very professional and friendly.

Rachel thought that outdoor weddings were very romantic. When Daniella told her the location for the wedding, Rachel said that it would also be a perfect location for beautiful wedding photos.

Rachel had her assistant determine the exact time that the sun would set on the wedding date. Her staff made all of the preparations around that time. Rachel used flowers and lights to create a simple but gorgeous aisle. The flowers matched Daniella's lily of the valley bridal bouquet. There was an arch made of colorful balloons to frame Andre and Daniella as they said their wedding vows.

When the wedding day came, the weather was perfect and everything flowed smoothly. There were strings of lights around the trees and citronella torches around the yard. All of the wedding guests were very impressed. Several parking attendants kept the flow of guests organized. Rachel even thought of heel covers and cement blocks for the bridal party to stand on so that their shoes wouldn't sink into the grass.

Daniella wore a white lace gown. Her bridesmaids wore aqua chiffon dresses and carried blue peonies. Andre wore a white tuxedo. His best man and groomsmen wore black tuxedos with aqua bowties, cummerbunds, and boutonnieres. One of Hendrix's customers was a judge and he officiated the wedding.

The reception was inside a large white tent with enormous ceiling fans hanging down. The tent accommodated 100 guests for a formal dinner. There was also a dance floor, band, and a photo booth area. The tables were adorned with ivory linen, real china, silverware, and glassware. The guests were offered delicious appetizers, which they were able to enjoy while dancing, listening to music, looking at the surrounding lake, or relaxing at the tables. The reception menu included black sea bass, chicken, beef tenderloin, and steamed fresh vegetables. The wedding cake was three-tier chocolate with vanilla buttercream icing.

During the reception, Andre and Daniella thanked their guests and stated, "It was overwhelming to share our wedding with everyone we loved. This was the wedding of our dreams. I want everybody to enjoy the evening and dance the night away!"

At that moment, there was a great firework display that lit up the sky. It was a picturesque moment that no one would ever forget. During the reception, my mother announced, "Dan Hendrix is staring at you." I told her, "You are seeing things."

I had decided to go back to college and combine two of my passions—my love for music and children. I wanted to become an elementary school music teacher. I applied at the Albany College of Fine Arts where Andre was on staff. My mother was excited about the decision to go back to college and offered to pay the tuition.

While filling out the admission paperwork, I had to list two people as emergency contacts. I wrote down my mother's name first and Andre's second. The admission clerk noticed Andre's name and told me I was eligible for a tuition reduction since I was related to one of the academia. Andre didn't know about the tuition assistance, but upon hearing about it he was glad.

A few weeks after Andre and Daniella came back from their honeymoon, Daniella invited me to lunch. She shared their honeymoon adventures and I told her my news about going back to college. Daniella suggested, "Come live with Andre and me."

I told Daniella, "It is a nice invitation, but I would not be so inconsiderate. You are newlyweds and don't need anyone living with you at this time." I insisted that I would be fine living on campus.

Daniella asked me, "Will you ever get married again?"

I told her it never entered my mind so I was not sure. She then surprised me by asking, "Can my brother, Dan, call you?" I responded, "Okay." I was curious why Dan would want to call me.

I changed the conversation by asking Daniella, "How did the Hope is Here Ministries began?" Daniella explained that Hope is Here Ministries was founded by Pastor Ronald Redding and their goal was to stop human trafficking by providing awareness and education.

All volunteers are shown an introduction video of Pastor Redding's niece, Brenda. She gives her testimony of being a rebellious teenager who spent a lot of time with Pastor Redding and his wife when she was more than her parents could handle. When she was fifteen years old, she had met an eighteen-year-old boy. He seemed nice but was hiding a serious drug addiction. Soon, he introduced Brenda to drugs, and she began skipping school and staying out late at night.

Her parents sent her to a drug rehabilitation center, but she soon ran away. She would send postcards from different cities telling her parents she was doing okay. Brenda tried other rehab programs and eventually became homeless. Eventually, her drug-addicted boyfriend abandoned her.

She finally found a center that helped her to become drug-free. Once Brenda became sober, she began to notice things that didn't seem right. She and other residents were always moved around to deplorable locations where there were always different faces. Brenda started asking questions but always got vague answers. She had a sense of danger, so one day she pretended to be sick so she wouldn't be moved. Brenda was able to escape and find a payphone to call her parents.

They were able to locate where she was and rescued her. Several months later, they found out that she had been involved with a human trafficking network. Pastor Redding told her that the church had been praying for her safe return.

I told Daniella, "I want to know more." She suggested I attend the next Hope is Here Ministries weekly meeting.

Later that night, I read the Hope is Here Ministries pamphlet that Daniella found in her purse. To my surprise, the founder was the pastor that I had watched that night in the motel room. I started reading the information:

Human trafficking generates profits up to $32 billion per year; sex trafficking accounts for 58% of all human trafficking cases that are investigated around the world, and labor trafficking accounts for 36%. Women account for 55 to 60% of the victims and girls, under the age of eighteen, account for 75% of trafficking victims. Children account for 27% of the victims. Two out of every three child-trafficking victims are girls.

100,000 to 300,000 American kids under the age of eighteen are involved in prostitution annually and are often targeted by sexual predators. The average age of a child sexually exploited is eleven. The average age of entry for a girl into prostitution is thirteen, but for a boy, the age is twelve. Victims of human trafficking have a short average life span of seven years. With less than 1% of the victims being rescued, they are more likely to escape trafficking by suicide or murder than by way of escape. The reason why rescue is so rare is that once a girl is trafficked, she becomes both a hidden and a moving target for anyone seeking to rescue her.

I'd had no idea that human trafficking was this bad. Once I read that Washington, D.C. was one of the cities where human trafficking is the worst, I decided to visit the New York office of Hope is Here Ministries and become a volunteer. When I walked in, the first thing I noticed was a map of everywhere someone had been rescued. The map also identified places where women and children were still being held captive.

My first assignment was to stuff envelopes with letters asking for monetary donations. I started thinking about all the wealthy clients that my mother and David had and how they could be potential untapped donors. Immediately, I started compiling a list of other potential donors, such as Mr. Jackson and his father's fellow pastors, Hendrix's customers, Mr. Green and his contacts, and former school and college alumni. Then I had the idea of having a musical benefit concert to raise additional monies.

After my volunteer shift ended, I called Daniella and asked her what she thought about the idea. She was just as excited as I was. The two of us decided to approach Pastor Redding together and asked him what he thought of a benefit concert. Pastor Redding gave his approval, blessing, and gratitude.

Daniella asked Andre and Dan if they would help us organize the concert. They both said that they knew a lot of performers who might be interested in performing for the benefit concert. The four of us started planning. Andre made a request to use the college's auditorium for the concert, which seats 1,000 people. We agreed to charge $1,000 a ticket for the concert. Andre and Dan were in charge of soliciting performers. Daniella and I took care of the advertisement, invitations, and the programs.

Daniella suggested for Andre and me to do a duet. I explained that I hadn't performed in public since high school. Andre started bragging about how talented I was. He told Daniella and Dan about the musical I wrote in high school and that it had been performed at a community theatre for an entire summer. With complete surprise, I asked Andre how he knew that.

He explained, "Aunt Lottie told me while I was down in Louisiana. I had wanted to know what you had been doing since the last time I saw you at our father's funeral."

In my final defense I said, "There is a difference between writing and performing. Why don't Andre and Daniella sing a song together?"

Andre told me, "Dan and Daniella were already playing a song together to accompany Mrs. Hendrix who is coming out of retirement for the concert." They finally persuaded me to perform.

While growing up, Dan and Daniella were encouraged by Mrs. Hendrix to appreciate different genres of music. Dan and Daniella decided to be classical musicians. During our planning meetings for the concert Andre, Dan, and I had debates about classical music versus jazz. Since Andre was a teacher of music, he usually started the debate.

Daniella finally spoke up to bring all the debating to an end saying, "Differences among all kinds of music are to be celebrated. Regarding classical and jazz, neither is inferior to the other in any way. The key for both classical and jazz is the fact that both must be performed from the heart and soul."

Chapter 6 : Second Chance For Love

During one of our final meetings together to discuss the performance lineup, Andre stated he had an idea. He said that we could sing together *My Angel Ray*, the song that our father wrote when I was a baby. I agreed to do it in remembrance of our father.

This concert was the first time Mrs. Hendrix, Dan, and Daniella had ever performed together. When Mrs. Hendrix's fans heard she was coming out of retirement for this benefit concert, the tickets sold very fast. They received several standing ovations after their performance.

Before Andre and I sang, he did a little introduction. He spoke about our Papa and conveyed that this was the only song that he had ever written. When we completed the song, we received a standing ovation also. Daniella and Dan came on stage with a bouquet of roses. They informed the audience that the concert was my idea.

The concert was a huge success; we raised over one million dollars. Pastor Redding was speechless when we presented the check to him. The concert also caught the attention of the media. Several radio and television stations interviewed Pastor Redding.

Two weeks after the concert, Dan called and invited me to a restaurant that had just opened. After eating a delicious meal, we talked until closing time. Dan had always seemed shy, but he was funny, intelligent, sensitive, and romantic. He invited me out again on Sunday. Dan told me, "You don't have to dress up, just wear something casual."

For our next date, Dan took me to church. Pastor Ronald Redding was the senior pastor at this church called House of

Prayer for Eternity. I felt genuine love from the church greeters as soon as we walked through the doors.

We went to brunch after church to talk. Dan explained, "One night when I couldn't sleep, I was flipping through television channels and heard Pastor Redding. His voice captivated me and I felt like Pastor Redding was talking directly to me." I agreed with Dan and shared that I had felt the same way. After being a part of the fundraiser for Hope is Here Ministries and hearing his sermon, I knew that I needed to attend another church service. I explained to Dan that the only other church I ever attended was my Aunt Lottie's.

I told him, "It was a much different experience. Aunt Lottie's church focused more on denominational doctrine. Both the attire of the congregation and the genre of worship music were different. I remember while planning for my wedding, having a rude conversation with the church secretary. She had quoted an exorbitant amount of money because we were not members of the church. When Aunt Lottie found out, she called that church secretary and told her that I was her grand-niece. The secretary's attitude changed because Aunt Lottie and Uncle Claude were well respected in that church. There was to be no alcohol served at the reception. So after the reception, we had an after-party at my mother's house for the bridal party, close friends, and family."

Another unusual date with Dan was when we visited a nursing home. Dan wanted to see his and Daniella's first music teacher, Mrs. Clara Jefferson. Dan explained, "Five of Mrs. Jefferson's former music students and I take turns visiting her at the home. Mrs. Jefferson has dementia."

Chapter 6 : Second Chance For Love

The day we went, all of the residents were in the community room playing bingo. Dan said, "I found out by trial-and-error that bingo day was the best time to visit her. She becomes very talkative and seems to reminisce more." I used to play bingo with Aunt Charlotte and her friends. Mrs. Jefferson noticed how I played multiple cards at one time and was the first one to yell bingo.

Mrs. Jefferson asked me, "How did you learn to play so good?" I told her about my Aunt Charlotte. Mrs. Jefferson said, "I had a best friend name Charlotte, but everyone called her Lottie." I shared that was the same name my family called Aunt Charlotte. Mrs. Jefferson asked me, "Where were you born?" I replied, "Washington, D.C., but my father's family is from Louisiana."

It turned out that Mrs. Jefferson was from Louisiana, and we were talking about the same Lottie. Mrs. Jefferson's husband had been in the army too. His last duty station was in New York. She had no other family.

Mrs. Jefferson had always wanted children. She also wanted to be a music teacher, but all their traveling with the army stopped that idea. Her husband suggested that she teach private lessons instead.

Mrs. Jefferson took Dan and me to her room after the bingo game. She kept a scrapbook of all her students and their accomplishments. Dan tried to cover up the picture which showed a younger version of himself. We all laughed. Dan said, "Mrs. Jefferson told each one of her students that they were her favorite student."

Mrs. Jefferson said, "I always wanted to make everyone feel special." As Dan and I left, Mrs. Jefferson gave me a big hug and told me to tell Aunt Charlotte hello. I told her I would.

A few months after Andre and Daniella had been married, she announced to Dan, "I don't want to travel and perform concerts after our contract is up." Dan understood and said he was tired of traveling also. He planned to play his violin for the local symphony orchestra. They had been after him to join them for years.

Dating Dan was a new experience for me. It was an interesting courtship. When we went to the Hendrix family farm, Dan taught me how to ride a horse and milk a cow. I even saw a calf's birth.

We didn't have much of anything in common except our love for music. Dan had never really dated before. He had put so much time into his violin playing that he hadn't taken much time for a relationship. However, this was good because we were learning different things together.

Since Dan was allergic to seafood and couldn't tolerate spicy foods, we learned to cook different dishes and Dan cooked for me a lot of times. We did not live together but we would plan our menu a week in advance and then shop for the ingredients and cook on Fridays. Tuesdays and Thursdays were Dan's rehearsal days. Those days, I volunteered at Hope is Here Ministries if I didn't have a lot of schoolwork or a test the next day.

Dan usually had concerts on Saturdays and Sunday evenings. On Wednesday nights we went together to Bible study. Those nights, Dan would pick up something from a deli and then pick me up from school. Sunday mornings we went to church together.

Chapter 6 : Second Chance For Love

We compromised on watching movies. Dan liked action and westerns, but he didn't like horror films. I introduced him to nostalgic black-and-white films. Dan had an oversized couch and large television in his living room. Most Fridays after cooking and cleaning, we would start watching a movie. Often we never finished watching it. The college was only approximately thirty minutes away by taxi, but sometimes I spent the night on the couch.

After attending church for three months, we decided to become members. Attending a new member's orientation was a requirement to becoming a member. At the orientation, we were able to get all of our questions about the church answered. A year later, on a Friday evening after cleaning up the kitchen, we sat on the couch to watch a movie. Dan said, "I've borrowed a videotape from a friend." I was intrigued because it was a black-and-white movie. Dan explained it was about a young man who decides to ask his girlfriend to marry him."

I started to notice that the voices I heard didn't match the actor's lips on the screen. I was surprised when the characters' names were Dan and Raynelle. Dan's friend had technically done a voiceover with the tape. He used Dan's voice asking me to marry him through the actor in the movie. After laughing for a few minutes, I said, "Yes! This was the most ingenious way to propose to someone!"

We decided to receive marriage counseling from Pastor Redding. He started our initial meeting with prayer. Pastor Redding stated, "All participants first have to fill out a pre-marital counseling questionnaire. I use the questionnaire to determine the topics to be discussed during the marriage counseling session. The eight-hour session will be on the first Saturday of the next month. We will have two fifteen-minute breaks and a one-hour lunch break."

Dan and I signed a commitment contract promising that they would be on time and answer all the questions with complete honesty. Pastor Redding also ended the meeting with prayer. He told us once we had completed the questionnaire we could mail it back to him or drop it off at the church office. Dan and I thanked Pastor Redding for his time. Dan took me to my dorm and then he went home.

With excitement, I couldn't wait to start filling out the questionnaire. This was the first step to becoming Mrs. Raynelle Hendrix. I repeated it again—Mrs. Hendrix. I liked how that sounded out of my mouth. However, after the initial introduction to the questionnaire, my excitement soon turned to disappointment as I started filling it out.

This survey is designed to help the counselor, Pastor Redding, understand who you are, where you're at in your current relationship and your view of love and marriage. Some of the questions seemed to be a bit threatening. He had told us, "Please be assured that your answers will be held in strict confidence and will be used to help you establish a more solid foundation for your marriage. This survey will only be useful to the extent that you answer the questions honestly and thoughtfully. Please answer the questions by yourself, without discussing your answers with your proposed partner. May the Lord bless you as you seek to establish a greater understanding and a better knowledge of marriage."

The questions started to bring back old memories. Concerned, I called Dan and asked him, "Have you looked at the questionnaire?"

"No," was his response. "I was hungry and began to fix myself a sandwich."

I informed him, "The questions were very personal."

Dan said, "I think that is the whole point of it."

"Okay, Dan," I said. "Please read through the questionnaire and then call me back." Dan agreed.

One hour passed. Then two hours. I called Dan back again. "I thought you were going to call me back after you read through the questions?"

Dan said, "I thought you wanted me to call you back after I finished filling it out. I'm sorry Raynelle, I misunderstood you."

I asked him, "Did you find the questions too personal?"

"Yes, they are personal, however, I feel that they identify topics that are really important for a successful marriage. Raynelle, I want to be married to you for the rest of my life. There is no one else on this earth that I want to spend the rest of my life with and eventually be the mother of my children. I think there are areas of marriage we haven't discussed and this pre-marital counseling will help us do just that. I feel we need to start our marriage with no secrets." I understood what he was referring to and I loved him even more for not saying it out loud.

Dan told me, "If you feel uncomfortable about the pre-marital counseling then we won't do it."

"No, we will still do it," I replied.

"Okay, I will talk with you again tomorrow."

With tenderness, I said, "I love you, Dan."

He replied, "I love you too, Raynelle."

I put my feelings and emotions aside and finished filling out the questionnaire. I had to take small breaks because some of the questions brought back painful memories and caused me to cry and get angry.

When I finally finished the questionnaire it was past one o'clock in the morning. I placed it in a sealed envelope to give to Pastor Redding before the weekly Bible Study.

Dan and my schedules were extremely busy the weeks before we were to meet with Pastor Redding again. Pastor Redding used our answers to the questionnaire to draft the topics that we would discuss. Pastor Redding started the session with a prayer like that of our initial meeting.

> *Dear Heavenly Father, I thank you for this day of new mercy and grace. Father, I lift up this pre-marital session with Dan and Raynelle.*
>
> *Father, I pray for wisdom and guidance for me. Father, I pray for Dan and Raynelle to have a receiving heart to your Holy Word as we together study your purpose and plan for their marriage. I thank you now for a loving and devoting marriage between Dan and Raynelle.*

We all said, "Amen!"

Pastor Redding stated, "It is a privilege that I am your shepherd, and it's my responsibility to explain the covenant of marriage according to God and His Word. I am also going to share my thirty-two years of experience of being a husband and father."

Pastor Redding explained, "You and Dan are two separate individuals coming together to make one couple. Becoming one couple doesn't mean losing your identity as an individual, but working together to accomplish Gods' purpose in your marriage." Pastor Redding read:

> *But "God made them male and female" from the beginning of creation. "This explains why a man shall leave his father and his mother and is joined to his wife, and the two are united into one." Since they are no longer two but one, let no one split apart what God has joined together.*
> *-Mark 10:6–9*

He further explained, "With God, you will be like a three-strand cord intertwined to make one strong rope. With God, His Word, and the three Cs, you will have a successful marriage. The three Cs begin with communication—talk, converse, and exchange information between the two of you. There is a difference between hearing and listening. Hearing is the act or process of perceiving sounds. When you listen you make the conscious effort to hear and pay close attention with clear understanding." Pastor Redding read from the Gospel of James to emphasize this:

> Understand this, my dear brothers and sisters: You must all be quick to listen, slow to speak, and slow to get angry.

Human anger does not produce the righteousness God desires.
    -James 1:19–20

Pastor Redding said, "The second is compromise—to give-and-take, to yield, and to negotiate when you can't totally agree. He read, "A hot-tempered person starts fights; a cool-tempered person stops them." (Proverbs 15:18)

He further explained, "A time will come in your marriage where you will not agree on an issue. Before any disagreements become intense to the point where hurting words being said that may not be easily forgiven, you should retreat to determine a compromise. Individually, you should seek God and His Word then return calmer, clearer, and able to discuss what God has shared with you. When there is agreement between the two of you, then you have power against the devil and all evil." He read from the Gospel of Matthew:

> "Again I say to you that if any two of you agree on earth concerning anything they may ask, it will be done for them by My Father in Heaven. For where two or three are gathered together in My name, I am there in the midst of them."
>   -Matthew 18:19–20

Pastor Redding announced, "The third is commitment—promise, pledge, and devotion that no matter what, the vows that you make before God and to each other will be honored to have a successful marriage. Marriage is work. It is a relationship for life."

Pastor Redding said to Dan, "Your commitment to Raynelle must include love only for her because a woman needs protection and provision."

Then he told me, "Your commitment to Dan should include loving only Dan, believing that he will love, protect, and provide for you. You must always stand with him and support him."

Pastor Redding said, "I could tell from your answers to the questionnaire that you had already started applying the three Cs. You applied it when you chose where you were going to eat and the type of entertainment you would share. God compares marriage to Jesus Christ and His church." He referred to Ephesians:

> And further, submit to one another out of reverence for Christ. For wives, this means submit to your husbands as to the Lord. For a husband is the head of his wife as Christ is the head of the church. He is the Savior of His body, the church. As the church submits to Christ, so you wives should submit to your husbands in everything. For husbands, this means love your wives, just as Christ loved the church. He gave up His life for her.
> -Ephesians 5:21–25

Pastor Redding commented, "While looking over the questionnaire, I noticed that you were not raised in any type of religious setting. It was very good that you both had gone through the new member's class since joining the church. Are you still planning on attending this church after you are married?"

We both said, "Yes."

"I'm glad to hear that," he remarked. Pastor Redding asked, "Is there anything that you still have questions about concerning the church?" We both agreed that all our questions were answered during the new member's orientation.

"Raynelle, I see that you have just started back to college."

"Yes sir, that's right," I replied.

"Have you two discussed if your schedules will continue the way that they are after you get married?"

I stated, "I will move in with Dan until we decide to get another place and that won't be until I find employment."

I found out during the session that there had never been a divorce in Dan's family, even though most of his relatives had married young. Dan stated, "I never saw my parents argue."

"I wish my family had been the same way. Dan and his siblings tease their parents because of the many times his parents finish each other sentences. I witnessed that also with my Uncle Claude and Aunt Lottie."

Pastor Redding didn't go over some of the questions on the questionnaire because they had been covered during the new member's orientation. One of the topics was sex. Dan and I had agreed to abstain until we got married. We both wanted our first time together to be special because Dan had confessed he was still a virgin. Both of us were glad that Pastor Redding didn't bring up the topic of sex also because of an incident that had happened recently.

Chapter 6 : Second Chance For Love

Dan likes showers, but I enjoy long baths. One morning, after spending the night on the couch, he forgot to lock the bathroom door and I had walked in on him. Dan didn't see me, but I was embarrassed and quickly backed out of the bathroom. As I left the bathroom, I was thinking that he was very muscular.

During the session, I discovered that I had to overcome two complexes. I was taller than Dan and he was very affectionate. He liked to hug and kiss a lot. The entire Hendrix family was like that. Whenever we cooked together in the kitchen, I sat on a stool. Being self-conscious, Dan had purchased shoe lifts to make himself much taller. Rumor has it that some of Hollywood's greatest superstars also use them. The brand Dan choose were customizable, giving him the option to add from one to two-and-a-half inches to his frame. When Dan bumped himself up an inch, he didn't get many responses. However, when he slipped on the maximum shoe boost, his friends thought that he'd had a sudden growth spurt. Dan started feeling self-conscious. The shoe design he chose was a wedged heel not unlike those found in women's shoes. So Dan also felt a side effect of feeling wobbly; as if his center balance had suddenly been dislocated. It took him two days of walking to get his balance. He took a few private walks around the block before using them in his everyday life. Dan really liked slip-on shoes, but the lifts for more height worked better in lace-up shoes or boots. After a few weeks, Dan decided that they were not for him.

After the last fifteen-minute break, Pastor Redding stated, "I need to go over just one more thing. I see you set the wedding date for a week after Thanksgiving. I will have to check my calendar."

We told him, "There will be family only invited."

Pastor Redding hugged us and said, "It will be a privilege and honor to marry you. My secretary will call you both to finalize that the date you chose is available." We thanked him and left very happy.

My mother called to find out how the counseling session went. She had told me that it was a very good idea and David thought so too. I explained to her I had reservations about going. My mother said that they did too, but David and her still needed counseling, even though they had been friends long before they started dating and felt that they already knew each other. Hearing her say that made me happy that I went through with it.

Mr. and Mrs. Hendrix also thought it was a good idea that we were having counseling because both of us came from very different backgrounds. Mrs. Hendrix had told Dan, "This world system can be a strain on marriages by having so many issues and distractions."

The wedding was scheduled for the weekend after Thanksgiving. I wanted our wedding to be totally different from my first one. Only our families were invited to attend. The following week, Dan had a concert in Hawaii. He knew that I always wanted to visit Hawaii, so we flew there for our honeymoon and stayed another week after the concert.

The concert was for the memorial anniversary of the bombing of Pearl Harbor. The commemoration ceremony was held on the main lawn of the Pearl Harbor Visitor Center in Honolulu, Hawaii. The survivors that attended had come to pay their respect to the 2,400 soldiers who had died that day. A ninety-one-year-old survivor had been near the Pacific Fleet on Ford Island when Japanese planes flew overhead. Those planes started dropping bombs that claimed approximately 2,400 lives and marked the United States' first battle of World War II. On Oahu, this memorial day had approximately 2,500 guests sitting facing Pearl Harbor, where twenty-one vessels were sunk or damaged along with 323 military planes.

As the audience looked on, a Navy vessel sailed into the harbor and whistled at 7:55 a.m. to signal for a moment of silence at the exact time the attacks had begun. The keynote speaker stated, "By honoring our past, we inspire our future and ensure the events of that day will never be forgotten." The ceremony also included music by the Navy's U.S. Pacific Fleet Band, a Hawaiian blessing, a cannon salute by the U.S. Army, echo taps, and wreath presentations.

When Dan and I got back from our honeymoon, we began moving my things into his house. Dan noticed a box that was marked Raynelle's treasures. He asked me, "What is in the box?" I opened the box and showed him the photo album from my mother, the pendant that Mr. Jackson had made for me with the picture of my father inside, and the earrings that Mrs. Bowman gave me during the tri-celebration party. Dan laughed at the name. I told him what we had been celebrating and then he understood.

In the meantime, Andre and Daniella had decided to start a family. When Daniella didn't get pregnant after several months of trying, they decided to see a specialist. The specialist, Dr. Kirk, did a blood test and an endometrial biopsy to check the lining of Daniella's uterus. Dr. Kirk determined from the physical exam, tests, and medical history that Daniella had a pelvic inflammatory disease or PID. Dr. Kirk explained, "PID is an infection of a woman's reproductive organs. It is a complication often caused by some sexually transmitted diseases like Chlamydia or gonorrhea." Daniella didn't understand. Dan had taken her out of town to a clinic to get antibiotics for STDs after she had been raped.

Dr. Kirk explained, "Even though you treated the STD, it can still cause serious complications. The best option for Daniella is a laparoscopy, which is a procedure using a lighted instrument inserted through a small cut in the lower abdomen to allow me to reconstruct her internal reproductive organs."

Daniella asked, "What are the success rates for this surgery?" He said, "30% usually become pregnant one year after surgery, yet the success rate has been as high as 65%." Dr. Kirk admitted, "I can't be completely sure about you until I actually perform the surgery."

Daniella asked Andre what he thought. Andre told her, "It is your body, so you will have to choose. I will support with whatever your decision is. You know I will always love you whether we have children or not."

Daniella told Dr. Kirk that she needed more time to make her decision. Daniella told Andre, "It's time to tell my mother everything." Andre said, "I'll drive you up to the farm over the weekend." Daniella said, "No, I need to do this by myself. I'll stay overnight and come home on Sunday." Andre was reluctant but agreed.

Mrs. Hendrix was surprised when Daniella arrived by herself. Daniella had known that she would be alone with her mother. Mrs. Hendrix was quiet for a long time after Daniella told her about the rape, her visit to the clinic, and her infertility. Mrs. Hendrix started crying uncontrollably.

Daniella held her tight and cried with her. Mrs. Hendrix finally spoke and said, "I'm such a terrible mother. I knew that something was wrong. I should have pushed the issue. Wait until I see that Dan."

Daniella hugged her tight saying, "Momma, you are the best mother anyone could ever have. All my life you were there for Dan and me during all of our issues, illnesses, and problems. You showed us that we were just as special to you as Aiden and Ryan and you know how stubborn and independent Dan and I have always been. I was just too ashamed and embarrassed to let anyone know. I was afraid of what Dad and the boys would do to Jeff. Dan knew because he guessed it. Please don't blame Dan. You know how he has always been very protective of me. It would crush him if he knew that you were mad at him."

Mrs. Hendrix calmed down a little and told Daniella, "See? You need me now and I will be with you through this whole infertility event."

Daniella decided to have the surgery. "Momma, I can't change the past. Yes, maybe if I had gone to our doctor back then I wouldn't have this problem, but I can't dwell on the past. Every decision has consequences and I'm living with mine."

Daniella and I had lunch together at least once a month. It was now a year after her surgery and Daniella still wasn't pregnant. At lunch she said, "Dr. Kirk had suggested several options of fertilization. Andre had also told me that we could adopt one of the little girls that had been rescued from sex trafficking. He told me that we both had a lot of love to give."

I told Daniella, "There is also another option."

"What is that?"

I explained that Pastor Redding was having a guest speaker, Pastor O'Brien, on Sunday and that he had a gift of healing from God. I told her how several members had given their testimonies about their healings. One woman had two miscarriages and, after Pastor O'Brien prayed for her, she became pregnant within a month and now has twin boys. Another member had a bulging disc and it disappeared. Some had their arthritis pain relieved, others had their hearing restored, and so many more."

Daniella told me, "Pastor Redding's church is okay, but I'm not sure about this healing stuff."

I said, "Pastor Redding is the most loving and genuine person that I know. You and Andre have tried it man's way, now it is time to let God help you."

Daniella stated, "I will discuss it with Andre." The following Sunday, Andre and Daniella went to Pastor Redding's church. When Pastor O'Brien asked for all the women who were having infertility issues to come up for prayer, Daniella went up to the altar with tears running down her face.

The next month, Daniella invited me to have lunch at her house because she was waiting for a very important phone call. The phone rang and Daniella went into the kitchen to answer it. When she came back from the kitchen she was crying hysterically. I ran to her and asked what was wrong. It was hard for Daniella to talk.

She finally calmed down and told me, "That call was Dr. Kirk's office to confirm that I am pregnant." We both held hands, jumped, and screamed as we ran around the living room.

We both lost our appetite. It had been replaced with joy. I told Daniella that I was so glad that we were sisters and how good it was that we would be pregnant together. Upon hearing my words Daniella's mouth dropped open. Again, we held hands, jumped, and screamed as we ran around the living room. Then we stopped and hugged each other.

Biblical Character For Chapter Six

"Why are you cast down, O my soul? And why are you disquieted in me? Hope in God, for I will yet thank Him for the help of His presence."
 -Psalm 42:5

Pastor Redding, Elijah, And Elisha

Pastor Ronald Redding's Hope is in being a good pastor. The Bible gives the account of two men who had similar life events as Pastor Redding with Elijah (in 1 Kings chapters 17–19; 21:17–29; 2 Kings 1:3–2:14; and Luke 4:25–26) and Elisha (in 1 Kings 19:16–21; 2 Kings chapter 2; 3:11–20; chapter 4; 5:8–6:23; 6:31–7:2, 16–20; 8:1–15; and 9:1–7).

Pastor Redding, Elijah, and Elisha were men of God that made it a lifestyle to seek His guidance daily. Pastor Redding had a family crisis which led to him starting a ministry that effective many. Human and sex trafficking is a form of idolatry. Elijah and Elisha had their ministries for the same purpose, to rid the nation of Israel of idolatry (false gods).

The Story of Elijah

Elijah the Tishbite emerged as if from nowhere to become Israel's greatest miracle worker since Moses. Elijah was opposed to the accepted standards of his day when belief in many gods was normal. He appeared in the role of God's instrument of

Chapter 6 : Second Chance For Love

judgment upon a wayward Israel because of the nation's widespread idolatry.

After three dry years, God instructed Elijah to present himself before King Ahab and end the drought. Elijah challenged Ahab to a battle of the prophets—a contest between one prophet of God and the 450 prophets of Baal on Mount Carmel. Ahab accepted the challenge. It was decided that each side would cut up a bull, lay it on wood with no fire, and then call on their god to take the offering by fire.

The ceremony began in the morning with the appeal to Baal. By noon, after Ahab's prophets had repeatedly cried out, "O Baal, answer us!" there was still no fire. Elijah laughed at them with jokes that perhaps Baal was meditating, on a journey, or sleeping. Baal's prophets became agitated. To get the attention of their god, they slashed themselves with their swords until they were covered with blood.

When there was still no response, the time came for the afternoon sacrifice, and the spectators turned their attention to Elijah. He built an altar with twelve stones to represent the twelve tribes of Israel, laid the wood and the sacrificial bull on the altar, and dug a deep trench around it. He had twelve jars of water poured over the sacrifice and the wood until the altar was saturated and the trench was overflowing. Then Elijah stood by the altar and said, "O Lord, God of Abraham, Isaac, and Israel, let it be known this day that you are God in Israel." The fire of God consumed not only the pieces of the bull but the wood, the stones, the dust, and even the water in the trench. The people were astounded and acknowledged Elijah's God as Lord. They seized the false prophets, who were then executed by Elijah in accordance with Jewish law. Elijah then announced that God would end the drought. He prayed seven times for rain with his face humbly between his knees. When a little storm cloud appeared on the horizon, Elijah ran down the mountain to the city to announce the coming of the rains.

The prophet Elijah did not die. He was carried bodily to heaven in a whirlwind. This was an honor previously bestowed only upon Enoch. Elisha, the only witness to this event, picked up Elijah's mantle which fell from him as he ascended. He carried it during his ministry as a token of his continuation of Elijah's ministry.

The Story of Elisha

Elisha was the prophet Elijah's successor. While Elijah's ministry was intense and aggressive, Elisha's was gentler. Elijah's life had solitary, but Elisha was oriented around people and often lived with groups of other prophets. Elisha's entire ministry was mingled with government affairs, advising and anointing kings, and warning his country of imminent danger. He not only predicted future kings, but he also anointed new rulers and foresaw military defeats and victories.

Before taking his leave, Elijah fulfilled the final request of Elisha by providing him with a double portion of his prophetic spirit, making him his spiritual firstborn. Upon receiving Elijah's mantle, Elisha demonstrated this gift by parting the waters of the Jordan River, allowing him to cross on dry land. In this way, Elisha demonstrated that he had received God's blessings on his ministry as Elijah's successor.

Elisha cultivated a different image from his predecessor. Instead of following Elijah's examples as a loner and an outsider, Elisha chose to work within the established system. He assumed his rightful place as the head of the official prophetic order in Israel where his counsel and advice were sought out by kings. In contrast to Elijah's strained relationship with the king and his officials, Elisha enjoyed the harmonious role of trusted advisor. This is not to say that Elisha never had a word of criticism for the government; he did play a part in the overthrow of Jezebel and the dynasty of Ahab.

Perhaps the most important part of his ministry, however, was how Elisha followed in Elijah's footsteps. This consisted of his performance of miracles which answered a wide variety of needs in every level of society. He had a reputation for sympathizing with the poor and the oppressed. Elisha's activities and miracles as a prophet were often focused on those who were abused by officials in positions of power.

One of Elisha's community service miracles was his purification of an unhealthy spring near Jericho. After learning that the spring was bad, Elisha threw a bowl of salt into it making it pure. In another miracle, Elisha helped the widow of one of the sons of the prophets. To help her pay off creditors who intended to take the widow's two sons as payment, Elisha multiplied the amount of oil in one jar to fill all available containers. This brought in enough money to pay off the debts and provided a surplus on which the widow and her sons could live.

Elisha also advised kings and performed miracles for them. He helped Jehoram, the king of Israel, and Jehoshaphat, the king of Judah. He also helped the king of Edom defeat Mesha, the king of Moab. Elisha ministered to all people regardless of their nationalities. He cured Naaman, the commander of the Syrian army, of leprosy, but he also advised the king of Israel of the plans of their Assyrian enemies.

Even the bones of the deceased Elisha had miraculous powers. When a corpse was hidden in Elisha's tomb, it came back to life when it touched the prophet's bones.

> "My soul longs for Your deliverance, but I Hope in Your Word."
> -Psalm 119:81

Brenda Redding And The Prodigal Son

Brenda Redding found Hope was in that she could share her testimony and help others. The Bible gives the account of a prodigal son (in Luke 15:11–32). This Biblical character has similar life events as Brenda. Brenda and the prodigal son both were raised in homes that taught the Word of God. So often, we feel our way is better than our parents and then consequences prove differently.

Brenda's disobedience led to her purpose in life. Through her uncle's ministry, Brenda helped those caught in human and sex trafficking. She learned not to judge God's ultimate intentions for her life based on current circumstances. The prodigal son had to hit rock bottom to remind him of the Hope and love he had back home. God will always turn our mess into a message if we surrender our will to Him. We are more than conquerors through Christ Jesus.

Chapter 6 : Second Chance For Love

The Story of the Prodigal Son

The prodigal son was not so named in the Bible, but he was the foolish son who received his early inheritance and subsequently squandered it on wild living in another country. When a famine hit, he got a job feeding pigs in the field. His hunger was so great that he even craved their food.

This prodigal son realized that even his father's hired men had food to spare. He longed for home and determined to return and find work as a servant. The repentant son expressed how unworthy he was to be his father's son. His father embraced him with unconditional love, forgiveness, and restored him into the family in spite of his brother's objections.

This parable is meant to convey the attitude of forgiveness that God expresses to those who repent of their sins. The prodigal son was reckless and extravagant. When Jesus told the parable of the two lost sons, he devoted the first part of the story to the younger son who wasted his possessions with prodigal living. The lesson of the prodigal son is that when one abandons his father's house to venture into the far country, he ends up with an empty purse, an empty stomach, and a starving soul.

> "Now may the God of Hope fill you with all joy and peace in believing, so that you may abound in Hope, through the power of the Holy Spirit."
> -Romans 15:13

Daniella, The Shunammite Woman, and Hannah

Daniella Duplantier found Hope in the medical technology needed to assist her in conceiving a baby. The Bible gives the account of two women who had similar life events as Daniella with the Shunammite woman (in 2 Kings 4:8–36) and Hannah (in 1 Samuel 1:1–2:11).

Daniella, the Shunammite woman, and Hannah were women who longed to have children. Each one of these women received their miracle sons through prayer. These miracles demonstrated that God is the God of the impossible for those who believe. Many time, the answer to our prayers don't come right away, but a delay is not a denial. God has His appointed time for all His promises.

The Story of the Shunammite Woman

The Shunammite woman was a female inhabitant of Shunem who befriended the prophet, Elisha. This third unnamed woman in the Book of Kings was not a widow but a childless wife. She was a respected member of her community. As Elisha, the prophet, often passed by her home, this woman had her husband prepare a special room where Elisha could stay for the night.

Later, when Elisha asked the woman what he could do for her, she had no request. However, Elisha's servant Gehazi observed that the woman was childless and that her husband was old. When Elisha announced that she would have a son, the woman responded, "No, Man of God, do not lie to your maidservant!" It wasn't that she didn't want a son, but she had determined to be satisfied with what life had provided. She feared she would make herself miserable if she hoped for what she thought she could not have. For those who have tried to isolate themselves from hurt by determining not to dream, the sudden introduction of hope can be frightening.

The child was born as Elisha had promised, but sometime later, the boy suffered from sunstroke and died. After her son died, the woman immediately set out to get Elisha. The Shunammite woman had chosen to live a life marked by the rejection of hope until Elisha appeared and gave her hope despite herself. Her hope had borne fruit. She had a son. However, now her son was dead, and in her dark despair, it seemed better to have lived the empty, hopeless life she had known before the boy was conceived than to experience the pain that now tore at her inmost being.

However, the Shunammite woman's story doesn't end there. Elisha's God restored the child to life and to his mother's arms. From this, the woman learned an important lesson about life. What was the lesson?

We may, like the Shunammite woman, reason that if we want nothing, we cannot suffer from its lack. If we have nothing, we cannot be hurt by its loss. However, such a life is empty. God invites us to live in hope and expectation rather than in hopelessness. While it is true that living in hope may bring us an unexpected pain and that every gain brings with it the possibility of loss, the God who guards and guides us is gracious indeed. In opening our lives to whatever the future may be, whatever pain we know will be more than balanced by His joy.

The Story of Hannah

Hannah was a woman longing for a child and living in a culture where barrenness is considered punishment for some dark, hidden sin. She was ridiculed by her husband's second wife.

During her family's annual trip to worship in the sanctuary at Shiloh, she pleaded with God for a child and vowed that she would dedicate him to the Lord. Hannah was praying with such emotion that Eli, the priest, accused her of drunkenness. He did not understand that she was pouring out her soul before the Lord.

Hannah conceived and gave birth to a son, Samuel, who later became Israel's first prophet. This child was Hannah's sign that God had heard and cared. Hannah kept her vow, and when the boy was weaned, she took him to the sanctuary to live with Eli and learn from him. Hannah brought both her child and her gratitude to God.

Throughout history, Hannah has been honored both as Samuel's mother and as a woman of faith. Hannah's life portrays how setting our hearts on something we do not have can rob us of appreciation for the gifts God has given us. It was only when Hannah surrendered the object of her desire to God that she found release from her anguish and discovered peace.

Chapter 6 : Second Chance For Love

Acknowledgements

All praise and honor go to ABBA Father! Without Him, this book would not be possible. With His inspiration, I was able to pour out my heart, mind, and soul. With His love, I learned where Hope comes from. I pray that this book will also help you to learn where your Hope comes from.

I would like to recognize my fifth-grade teacher, Mrs. Lewis. Mrs. Lewis always encouraged her students to show creativity in learning our spelling words. We had contests to see who could write the best story using all of our spelling words correctly. It was a very inventive learning tool.

I give thanks especially to my closest and dearest friend, Tiffany. She was the first person to suggest that I write a book. Tiffany is a true example of friendship. We have cried together, laughed together, and prayed together.

ABBA Father has blessed me with two prayerful spiritual moms. These women continually pray for me and my family. Many thanks to Ruth and BJ who have demonstrated love and given Hope to so many people.

I am forever grateful to my spiritual mentor, Apostle Donald Downing. His wisdom and authorship were an inspiration for me. He is the author of thirty-two books.

I recognize the many friends who have been my prayer partners.

My sincere gratitude for the professionalism of Alesha Brown and Fruition Publishing Concierge Services.

Salvation Prayer

If you don't know Jesus as your Savior and Lord, simply pray the following prayer in faith and Jesus will be your Lord!

> Heavenly Father, I come to you in the name of Jesus. Your Word says, "Whosoever shall call on the Name of the Lord shall be saved" and "If thou shalt confess with thy mouth the Lord Jesus, and shalt believe in thine heart that God hath raised Him from the dead, thou shalt be saved" (Acts 2:21; Romans 10:9).
>
> You said my salvation would be the result of Your Holy Spirit giving me new birth by coming to live in me (John 3:5–6, 15–16; Romans 8:9–11) and that if I would ask, you would fill me with your Spirit and give me the ability to speak with other tongues (Luke 11:13; Acts 2:4).
>
> I take You at Your Word. I confess that Jesus is Lord and I believe in my heart that you raised Him from the dead. Thank you for coming into my heart, for giving me your Holy Spirit as you promised, and for being Lord over my life. Amen.

Bibliography

Charisma Media/Charisma House Book Group. *The Kenneth Copeland Word of Faith Study Bible, Modern English Version.* Florida: Passio Publisher, 2017.

Esquire.com. "We tried it: shoe lifts-shoes for short men." New York: Hearst Corporation, 2013.

Freeman, Michael A.. *Marriage Made EZ in 31 days.* Maryland: FIG Publishing, 2012.

Garvey, Joan B. and Mary Lou Widmer. Edited and updated by Kathy Chappetta Spiess and Karen Chappetta. *Beautiful Crescent—A History of New Orleans.* Louisiana: Pelican Publishing Company, Inc., 2014.

Gruen, Dietrich and Julia Pferdehirt, Anna Trimiew, Carol Troyer-Shank, Sue VanderHook. *Who's Who in the Bible.* Illinois: Publications International, Ltd, 1998.

Lyness, D'Arcy. "Taking Your Child to a Therapist." California: Kids Health Org., 2013.

Mahaney, Carolyn, Crosswalk.com.. "Titus 2: Express a Tender Love for Your Children." Virginia: Salem Web Network, 2007.

Nalkup, Jim. "12 Topics You Must Discuss Before Getting Married." New York: dr-jim.com, 2015.

Richards, Sue and Lawrence. Every Woman in the Bible. Tennessee: Thomas Nelson Publishers, 1999.

Senelick, Richard. "Burning in Feet: Causes and Treatments." New York: WebMD Magazine and Medicine Net, 2014.

Shapiro, Treena. "Survivors commemorate 73rd anniversary of Pearl Harbor attack." New York: Reuters News Agency, 2014.

Sobik, Jakub. "How We Work." United Kingdom: The Printed Word, Thomas Clarkson House, 2014.

Vine, W.E. and Merrill F. Unger and William White, Jr.. *Vine's Complete Expository Dictionary*. Tennessee: Thomas Nelson Publishers, 1996.

WebMD.com.. "Female Infertility: Causes, Tests, Signs, Treatments." New York: WebMD Magazine and Medicine Net, 2015.

WebMD.com.. "Miscarriage Symptoms, Causes, Diagnosis, and Treatment." New York: WebMD Magazine and Medicine Net, 2015.

WebMD.com.. "Pelvic Inflammatory Disease Symptoms, Causes, Treatments." New York: WebMD Magazine and Medicine Net, 2015.

Wikipedia.org.. "Ballston, Arlington, Virginia." California: Wikimedia Foundation, 2015.

Wikipedia.org.. "Louisiana Creole People." California: Wikimedia Foundation, 2015.

Word Publishing. *The Holy Bible, New Century Version.*

Tennessee: Thomas Nelson Publishers, 2003.

Youngblood, Ronald F. and F.F. Bruce, Herbert Lockyer, Sr. and R.K. Harrison.

Nelson's New Illustrated Bible Dictionary. Tennessee: Thomas Nelson Publishers, 1995.

About the Author

Evangelist Bridgette Michele Alfred has been married to Elder Tyrone Alfred for 30 years. She is the mother of four children (three daughters and one son): Cheraun, Tiffany, Tylisa, and Teon; the grandmother of four (three grandsons and one granddaughter): Deja, Dane, Dean, and Jaden; one son-in-law, Kelvin, and one daughter-in-law, Valerie. Evangelist Alfred has extended family with Alonzo, Timothy, Edna, Cindy Campbell, and their families.

Evangelist Bridgette was raised in Washington, D.C. She is a Desert Storm Vet and served in the U.S. Army for 15 years. She retired in 2014 from the United States Capitol Police, where she served for 24 years.

Evangelist Bridgette accepted Jesus Christ as her Lord and Savior at the age of 14 and received the baptism of the Holy Spirit with evidence of speaking in tongues in her early twenties.

She is currently writing for an online magazine, "Urban Sentinel", a daily Facebook page, "Hope Is Real Devotional," and has plans for writing several more books.

www.ingramcontent.com/pod-product-compliance
Lightning Source LLC
Chambersburg PA
CBHW071429070526
44578CB00001B/46